Greenwood Press Reprint.
1978.

11221

£14.50
DR
INT

Sir Thomas Beecham

DISCOGRAPHY

GREENWOOD PRESS, PUBLISHERS
WESTPORT, CONNECTICUT

Library of Congress Cataloging in Publication Data

Sir, Thomas Beecham Society.
  Sir Thomas Beecham discography.

  Reprint of the 1975 ed. published by The Society,
Redondo Beach, Calif.
  Bibliography: p.
  Includes indexes.
    1. Beecham, Thomas, Sir, bart., 1879-1961--Disco-
graphy.
[ML156.7.B43S6 1978]   016.7899'12   78-2261
ISBN 0-313-20367-9

In Memory Of

Dana Von Schrader

*Charter Member and Faithful Friend
of the Society*

Reprinted with the permission of the Sir Thomas Beecham
Society

Reprinted in 1978 by Greenwood Press, Inc.
51 Riverside Avenue, Westport, CT 06880

Printed in the United States of America

10 9 8 7 6 5 4 3 2 1

THE BEECHAM DISCOGRAPHY - AN INTRODUCTION
BY WARD BOTSFORD

"But damn it!", the violinist expostulated, "He *can't* conduct. He doesn't suffer. If you want to conduct you've got to suffer. *Anybody* knows that!" The man was sincere and by most lights perfectly right, too. He was talking, of course, about Sir Thomas Beecham, Bart., C.H.

Beecham never suffered. To begin with he was so filthy rich so why should he suffer?! No matter what the music — be it the smallest of Delius' dances or the greatest of Beethoven's symphonies Beecham believed in enjoying himself. In this he was completely unique. Not for him the Toscanini cat-o'-nine tails, nor yet the super suffering of Furtwängler or the "probing" of Walter, to say nothing of the "all business" of the modern conductor. No, no! When Beecham got up on a podium something magical happened. Before the baton came down the orchestra was all smiles and even the critics knew that this was an easy review to write. How we all enjoyed those Royal Philharmonic Orchestra concerts! There was always a mixture of the tried and true along with a piece that made us say... "Why didn't I know that piece by Dvorak (or Delius or Mozart or Bax or...) before?" Anyone who left a Beecham concert left with a grin on his face. Beecham wanted it that way. He would not conduct a piece if he didn't enjoy it.

There is a certain brand of critic that will tell you that Beecham didn't conduct Stravinsky or Berg because he couldn't read and understand their scores. Nonsense! As a matter of fact he *did* conduct Stravinsky — but not often because it was not music that he enjoyed himself. Yes, enjoyment was a prerequisite of a piece's appearance on a Beecham program. Fortunately, his tastes were very broad...broader I would say than that of any other conductor. He did not *discover* Mozart, of course, nor Handel or even Delius. And yet — and yet — if it were not for Beecham, I wonder....? In the 'thirties only Beecham was really conducting these masterpieces. To be sure, you heard K.550 and 551 frequently, but the earlier works? Hardly. And he not only conducted them, he knew *how* to conduct them. Beecham's readings were robust, they were brilliant, they were healthy, and they had a smile on their face.

The records in this discography are all smiles. I've heard every one of them over the course of the years. I own most of them and they are old and valued friends. If I were to retire to that mythical desert isle and had to choose I would unhesitantly reach for my Beecham.

As any good recording executive can tell you, when a conductor dies his records die with him. The public wants the work of those in the limelight, not those of a dead hand. So it has been with Toscanini, Walter, Cantelli, Weingartner, Schalk, Muck, Wood, and countless others and so it has been with Beecham. It is not merely that the public constantly demands new faces so much as the fact that styles change. I doubt that Toscanini's tirades would get by today, nor would the pleasantness of Bruno Walter, nor yet the selfless dedication to music that was Weingartner. But Beecham might just beat that general rule. In some ways the Englishman was a Conductor for All Seasons. Yet, unlike Toscanini he left no "school" of conducting. Unlike Walter he left no following of talent. And unlike Weingartner he wrote no scholarly treatise to be studied by a later generation. No, all Beecham had was — if it must be summed up in a word — *CHARM*.

A strange word to use to describe the recorder of three vastly different versions of the *MESSIAH*, a large piece of *ELEKTRA*, sections from Wagnerian operas, the two stellar opera recordings of all time: *ZAUBERFLÖTE* and *LA BOHEME*. Yet it was charm that made all of these recordings possible. The charm that could contradict himself into three different *MESSIAH*s and yet make each one a vivid experience to an open-minded person. The charm that could turn the colossal Strauss orchestral mechanism into something intensely human and objective. The charm that enabled him to get the best out of singers as highly talented and different as Roswaenge and Bjoerling and Lemnitz and de los Angeles while at the same time working with orchestras utterly unknown to him.

Of course that charm will be better understood when I mention the definitive recordings of such as *ESPAÑA, NINA, MORNING, NOON AND NIGHT IN VIENNA, NUTCRACKER* and *AIR DE BALLET*. These are all charming of course. I am particularly struck when looking over this discography at the small pieces Beecham has devoted time and energy to. How perfect in every way is *ESPAÑA*. And that *NUTCRACKER*! Who can talk of another performance in the same breath?! Or the Dvorak *SLAVONIC RHAPSODY* — who ever heard of it before Beecham? But lest the word become worn out let me dwell too on the high skill of all of these charming records. To play any of these works one needs a first-rate orchestra and this Beecham always had. Sometimes it was the Royal Philharmonic and sometimes it was the WPA orchestra of out-of-work musicians in New York. So astute a critic as Virgil Thomson could scarcely tell the difference between the two.

How did he manage? Who can say. He was unique. He was the greatest orchestral trainer we have ever seen. The London Philharmonic and the Royal Philharmonic, two of the great orchestras of the world, were his creations. Created, almost literally, in the proscribed six days allotted to creation. I heard the Rochester Philharmonic play under his baton with but two rehearsals and — for that concert — the Rochester Philharmonic was a great band. He knew how to communicate enthusiasm to his men in an easy, natural way. Great orchestras loved him. The Philadelphia Orchestra... surely the richest of all orchestras... once in my hearing refused to take a bow at a Beecham concert and contented themselves with cheering Beecham as loudly as the audience.

I have read that Beecham did not conduct Haydn well. H.C. Robbins-Landon, the Haydn scholar, lists some 1,000 mistakes in Beecham's conducting of the *CLOCK* Symphony — or maybe it was 1,500 mistakes. Mr Robbins takes my breath away. To count so high for one so young is indeed an accomplishment. No doubt H.C.R.L. prefers his Haydn pristine pure — in his own edition, of course! — conducted by conductor X in a pure, perfect and absolutely bloodless way. This *does* seem to be the accepted style since modern conductors have discovered musicology. Well, mistakes or no, Beecham's Haydn — to say nothing of his Mozart — is robust and one gets more of the guts of the score when listening to Beecham than the more modern homosexual performances I've heard. Beecham may be not only behind the times, he may well be ahead of them!

Sir Thomas will, I am certain, occupy an unique niche in the history of conducting. Part of this will be due to his innate talents — there is hardly a handful of conductors whose names can be mentioned in the same breath — but mostly it will be because of his contribution to the phonograph. This for two reasons. First, of course, there is the sheer bulk, which no other conductor (save Ormandy, if he continues for many more years!) is likely to match, much less surpass. Second, there is its amazing quality in toto.

There can be very little doubt that the great conductors of this century will be judged ultimately by their recordings. No one in his right mind will believe what a printed review says about Herr X's or Signor Y's greatness if Herr X's or Signor Y's records are below par. For phonograph records, like photographs, do not tell lies (not even little "white" ones prior to the development of tape editing in the late 1940's). Beecham, beginning some six and a half decades ago, left us literally hundreds of great recordings and amazingly few bad ones. And when one stops to ponder how little most of the other great conductors have recorded, one quickly realizes how important the Beecham documentation will be to future ages.

The conductor's art is, of course, a fairly new thing. It hardly existed before 1850, and even then it was in a primitive state. Among the important conductors who *never* recorded were such personages as Weber, Spohr, Berlioz, Nicolai, Wagner (all better known as composers, anyway), Mottl, von Bülow, Levi, and Richter. And everyone knows that the true measure of many other, more recent conductors is not to be had from their recordings for various reasons. But that is another story.

Since what follows is a chronological discography, a few prefatory words regarding the several Beecham "periods" may be in order.

FIRST PERIOD:
ACOUSTIC RECORDINGS, 1910-1919

The artistic quality of these is, by and large, very low. It is tempting to find an explanation for this, but not profitable. Many conductors — e.g., Muck, Nikisch, and Toscanini — made important contributions to the phonograph in the acoustic era. Why not Beecham? Although it is true that the printed word cannot always be trusted, it is difficult to discount the hundreds and hundreds of good reviews written about Beecham in those days. Also, I have spoken at length to several musicians who played under him in the "Beecham Orchestra" from 1910 to 1917, and to others who heard his concerts; one and all they recall his performances with a smacking of musical lips. My guess is that Beecham simply was not very interested in the medium in those far-off days. But even then he made a few good discs. Among the most interesting are the Mozart *ZAUBERFLÖTE* Overture and the *TIEFLAND* excerpts. The Odeon records are the most curious. It is possible that there were in fact more than those listed, and perhaps they will turn up someday. Also, others may not be conducted by Beecham at all; see the note on Mascagni's *CAVALLERIA*. All recordings were done for EMI and appeared on one or more of the EMI labels — Odeon, HMV, or Columbia.

SECOND PERIOD:
EARLY ELECTRICS, 1926-1933

By now Beecham had become a finished conductor. In this group of recordings the most important would be the first *MESSIAH* — a quite revolutionary reading — a marvelous *DON QUIXOTE* with the New York Philharmonic (Wallenstein and Piastro were the soloists), and the first of many Delius recordings. All of these were done for Columbia except for *DON QUIXOTE* which was released in the United States by Victor.

THIRD PERIOD:
LONDON PHILHARMONIC, 1933-1940

Beecham founded this orchestra, and he seems to have whipped it into peak shape within a few weeks — an amazing feat. To name the outstanding records from this period would be an impertinence. All recordings were done for Columbia with the exception of the several Sibelius Society volumes issued on Victor-HMV. Falling into this period, by the way, is the Berlin performance of Mozart's *DIE ZAUBERFLÖTE* — to my mind the most nearly perfect opera recording ever made.

FOURTH PERIOD:
LONDON PHILHARMONIC, ETC., 1942-1947

Except for the acoustics these are the least satisfactory of Beecham's recordings. The New York Philharmonic records were involved in a celebrated litigation because of their poor technical quality — although they are not bad musically. The LPO discs are of variable quality. The orchestra had passed out of Beecham's control and he was getting ready to leave it. Probably the best recording of this period was the Handel *GREAT ELOPEMENT SUITES*. The Philharmonic series was done for Columbia, and LPOs for Victor-HMV.

FIFTH PERIOD:
ROYAL PHILHARMONIC, ETC., 1947-1959

Two years short of his 70th birthday, Beecham duplicated his feat of founding the LPO by founding the RPO. To attempt something like this at his age was remarkable. To have achieved such results as he did simply staggers the imagination. In his last years he was to record — to mention only the large-scale works — two complete and completely different versions of *MESSIAH*, operas by Mozart and Puccini, a *CARMEN*, a *FAUST*, Handel's *SOLOMON*, and 13 Haydn symphonies. The sheer work load was incredible.

* * *

Non-commercial recordings are listed because of their considerable historic and musical interest, and they are a very real part of the Beecham legacy. The Beecham Society have done their utmost to assure that these performances are preserved and are engaged in a program of issuance of the best of them in order that they might reach the widest public. Certainly there are things of inestimable interest here, and they form a valuable supplement to the commercial recordings.

It is late in the day to praise Beecham. He was a great conductor. Nothing can change that. His recordings are his monument and a very secure monument at that. No other conductor put so much of himself into his recordings. Herein they are laid cheek to jowl, and they do reach. The music on them — *any* music — is to be enjoyed. It must appeal to the senses with directness. We must cry over it. We must rejoice in it. The emotions must be engaged or, whatever the noise is, it isn't music. Beecham knew this. He knew it uniquely. And that is why he remains the greatest of all conductors.

This discography, begun about 1955 and now updated and revised by the

Society, was nursed into adulthood by the ministrations of a great number of people. Their names follow — in no particular order — and I thank them one and all. But I would first and foremost like to thank James Lyons, past editor of the *AMERICAN RECORD GUIDE*. Jimmy printed the first draft of this work in innumerable issues of the old *ARG*. He died last year and I lost at once a friend, as good an editor as ever was, and we all lost a fine magazine. So let me dedicate this discography to Jimmy. He would have understood. And, in addition, my thanks to the following who helped me with the first two editions:

The Sir Thomas Beecham Society, especially Stanley Mayes, Nathan Brown, Tom Patronite, and Jack Saul; and, in England, Ralph Stone, Denham Ford, and Arthur Ridgewell.

The staff of Radio Station WQXR in New York City, and especially Martin Bookspan.

John McClure and Jane Friedman of Columbia Records.

Richard Mohr of RCA Victor Records.

John Coveney of Capitol Records.

Robert Reid of Capitol International.

David Bicknell of EMI, England.

The British Institute of Recorded Sound, especially Patrick Saul and George Wylie.

Derek Lewis of the British Broadcasting Company.

Roland Gelatt for giving me the idea in the first place.

Edward J. Smith, the well-known collector and unsung public benefactor.

Dr. William B. Ober.

Denis Vaughan.

Lady Shirley Beecham.

Philip L. Miller, *ARG* Senior Critic (and former chief of the Music Division, New York Public Library), without whose help this project positively could not have been carried out.

The Library of Congress, Washington.

Pound Ridge, N.Y.
June 1975

This new discography of Sir Thomas Beecham's recordings has been compiled by the Beecham Society, taking as a basis the two editions by Ward Botsford previously published in the *AMERICAN RECORD GUIDE* and *LE GRAND BATON*. Certain changes have been made in approaching this latest effort that we hope will serve to satisfy both the archivist and collector to the greatest extent possible without unduly favoring one over the other. The result we feel is a work that is readable and yet contains factual information arranged in a format for quick and easy reference.

Except for the acoustic recordings (which are listed in matrix number sequence) we have used an alphabetical-chronological format, with the various periods of Beecham's recording career delineated as follows:

Section I
    Acoustical recordings, 1910-1917
Section II
    Early Electrical Recordings, 1926-1932
Section III
    A. The prewar recordings for EMI (Columbia and Gramophone Co.), England, 1933-1940
    B. American Columbia recordings, 1942
Section IV
    The postwar recordings for Decca & EMI (Gramophone Co.), England, 1944-1952
Section V
    The recordings for Columbia (USA) and Philips (England), 1949-1958
Section VI
    The recordings for RCA (USA) and EMI (England), 1955-1959

A code number (A-   ) is assigned to each recording so that indices can reflect composer and work, artists who recorded with Beecham, as well as record label and number. In addition, contained at the beginning of Sections 3 and 4 are summaries of recording sessions in chronological sequence with reference to code numbers of the recordings made at those sessions. Due to the lack of complete detailed information on recording dates in other sections it was deemed inadvisable to attempt to summarize those as well; however, as the information becomes available the procedure may be accomplished for them also. Only commercially made recordings, whether released or not, are included in the first six sections. Factual information concerning specific recordings have been incorporated by the use of footnotes.

As to nomenclature, where there is a generally accepted English title for works in other languages it is given as such; only when confusion might result or where a work is best known in the title of the original language is it left untranslated. Numbers and key signatures are given where available and essential to identification. Musical terms, such as "Konzert" and "Sinfonia" are translated into English. Movements from suites, etc., are not normally titled except in certain instances where different couplings or issues in excerpted form have occurred, or where the complete work as generally heard is not issued. Casts for operas and other works with many soloists are abbreviated to include the principal soloists involved; reference is made to the bibliography for more complete listings.

As to the recordings themselves, the integrity of a 78 RPM issue is preserved; i.e., if a Mozart symphony included a filler on the final side of the set, that filler is shown as a part of the set as originally issued. With certain LP collections it has been easier to separate the contents into individual entries; however everything is, of course, indexed individually regardless of its format within the body of the discography. For 78 RPM recordings, the first column lists matrix (plate) numbers and date of recording where known; all known existing takes of each side are shown, whether published or not. Matrix numbers are listed in the order that they appear in the set or work, and are collected together for an individual work within a set under a reference to the heading. The second column lists English (Great Britain) issue numbers, and the third American (U.S.) issue numbers. Original 78 RPM issue numbers are separated from LP issues by a line. Due to space limitations it is not possible to list issue numbers in other countries except where they do not duplicate English or American issues. Only *manual* set numbers are shown for U.S. issues, although most were issued in one or two automatic sequences with [DM-] or [AM-] prefix. Where the set number is indented after a record number (i.e., in *X-92*), the record numbers are contained within the set. Most of the post-war 78 RPM recordings were also issued in 45 RPM format in the U.S., with a [WDM-] prefix in the case of RCA Victor sets, or [49-] prefix for singles. These numbers are shown only where there is no LP equivalent.

For original LP recordings, matrix numbers are not shown, for they have little significance due to tape remakes and reissues from new stampers. For post-1954 recordings, mono and stereo numbers are given separately; if a stereo number is given with an asterisk, the record was most likely available only in stereo, although some record companies phased out their mono equivalents earlier than others. The prefix [S-] is usually added to a mono number when the record was released in both mono and stereo. Stereo numbers follow mono numbers in the listing. Most users will be familiar with such terms as 2ss (two sides) and prefixes used for stereo recordings versus mono ones.

* * *

Section VII (B-) lists in chronological sequence all known (or alleged) non-commercial recordings of in-concert performances, films, talks, lectures, and other programs by and about Beecham. These are also indexed by work, performer and issue number in cases where private recordings of the performances have been published.

An arbitrary time limit was set on incorporation of new information (which continually arrives) so the discography could be completed rather than leaving it "in the drawer" waiting for that last scrap of information; if there are discrepancies which seem to violate any of the rules outlined above, it is perhaps due to lack of access to proper identification and/or ignorance of the compiler. Being by no means "definitive," it is hoped that interested users will assist in filling-in what gaps still remain, and correct the errors which inevitably creep into a work of this scope. Periodic supplements will be published to reflect new information and issues.

We would gratefully acknowledge the valuable assistance of all the persons, companies, and institutions that contributed their time and knowledge, without which this task could not have been completed. They are, in no particular order:

Michael H. Gray, of the Library of Congress, for his untiring efforts in tracking down elusive recording dates;
Paul Koernich, for supplying valuable information about the pre-war recordings of the London Philharmonic Orchestra;
Andrew L. Guyatt, for his lobbying to the various record companies for reissues of Beecham recordings;
and to the following who have contributed valuable services in many areas, our thanks go to:
John Watson, International Classical Division, EMI Ltd.; Historical Sound Recordings, Yale University Library; Brad Engel, Angel Records; Bobby Finn and Tina McCarthy, Columbia Records; Michelle Slater and Lois Fox, RCA Records, New York; Eric Hughes, B.I.R.S.; Malcolm Walker; Brian Rust; Jack Saul; Denis Vaughan; Bill Holmes; David Quackenbush; Richard Warren, Jr; Dale Reutlinger; Richard C. Burns; Stanley H. Mayes; Marcelo A. Montarcé; Dr. Malcolm T. Duff-Miller; Ward Botsford; Denham V. Ford; John Hamer; Thomas E. Patronite; Alan Denson;
and to those we may have inadvertantly missed, our apologies.

N. E. Brown,
Recordings Executive,
The Sir Thomas Beecham Society

El Cerrito, California
July 1975

ABBREVIATIONS FOR RECORD LABELS/COMPANIES

Ang.	Angel Records, U.S.A. (EMI affiliate)
AFRS	Armed Forces Radio Service (U.S.)
BBCTS	British Broadcasting Corporation Transcription Services (G.B.)
CBS	CBS Records, England
Cap.	Capitol Records, U.S.A. (former EMI affiliate)
Col.	Columbia Records, U.S.A.
Col.	Columbia Graphophone Company, England (prior to 1932)
Col.	Columbia Gramophone Company, England (EMI affiliate after 1932)
Decca	Decca Record Company, England
EJS	Edward J. Smith, New York, USA
Elect.	Electrola, Germany (EMI affiliate)
Encore	Encore Records, England (EMI affiliate)
Font.	Fontana Records, England (Philips affiliate)
Gram.	Gramophone Company, London
HMV	Gramophone Company (His Master's Voice), E.M.I., London
IGI	I Grandi Interpreti, distributed in USA by Bruno Walter Society
Lon.	London Records, USA (Decca affiliate)
Odeon	Odeon/Fonotipia, Milan, Italy
Odys.	Odyssey Records, USA (Columbia, USA affiliate)
Pick.	Pickwick Records, USA (former Capitol affiliate)
Phi.	Philips Company, England
RCA	RCA Records, England (RCA, USA affiliate)
Sera.	Seraphim Records, USA (Angel affiliate)
Turn.	Turnabout Records, USA (Vox affiliate)
UORC	Unique Operatic Recording Corporation, New York, USA
Vic.	Victor Record Company, USA (EMI affiliate until 1956)
Vox	Vox Record Company, USA
WRC	World Record Club, England (EMI affiliate)
WSA	Sir Thomas Beecham Society, USA

SECTION I - THE ACOUSTICAL RECORDINGS, 1910-1917[3]

Beecham Symphony Orchestra

Part 1 - Gramophone Company, London, 1910[Note 1]

A-1 OFFENBACH: Tales of Hoffmann: Doll's Song (1ss)   Δ
     (Caroline Hatchard, soprano)
          4340f   Gram. 03193

A-2 OFFENBACH: Tales of Hoffmann: Legend of Klesäk (1ss)   Kleinsach
     (Walter Hyde, tenor, and chorus)
          4341f   Gram. 02256
                         Gram. D-106

A-3 OFFENBACH: Tales of Hoffmann: Opening Chorus (1ss)
     (Beecham Chorus)
          4347f   Gram. 04505

A-4 OFFENBACH: Tales of Hoffmann: When Love is But Tender and Sweet (1ss)
     (Walter Hyde, tenor)
          4353f   Gram. 02257
                         Gram. D-106

A-5 STRAUSS,J.: Die Fledermaus: Overture (Abridged-1ss)   Δ
          4360f[II]   Gram. 0627
          381ac   Gram. C-431[4]

A-6 d'ALBERT: Tiefland: Orchestral Selection (1ss)[Note 2]
          4423f   Gram. 0626

Part 2 - Odeon Company, ca. 1912

A-7 (a) MASCAGNI: Cavalleria Rusticana: Intermezzo (1ss)
     (b) MENDELSSOHN: Songs Without Words: A Bee's Wedding (1ss)
          (a) 143001, Lxg 40 Odeon 0772[5]
          (b) 143000, Lxg 41

A-8 (a) MISSA, Edmund(1861-1910): Muguette: Entr'acte (1903) (1ss)
     (b) ROSSINI: William Tell Overture: March (1ss)
          (a) 143013, Lxg 39 Odeon 0795
          (b) 143027, Lxg 30

A-9 (a) MOZART: Marriage of Figaro: Overture (1ss)
     (b) WEBER: Oberon Overture (Abridged-1ss)
          (a) 76212, Lxx 3677   Odeon X-84
          (b) 76211, Lxx 3678

Note 1: Recording speed 80 RPM. It is thought that the Offenbach recordings
         were made during July, 1910; all these recordings in Part 1 were advertised
         and reviewed in Sound Wave & Talking Machine Record, London, Dec. 1910.

Note 2: Label does not credit Beecham as conductor; orchestra only given.
         However, Beecham did perform the work at Covent Garden around this
         time (A Mingled Chime, pp. 162-3) so it is not unlikely he also
         conducted the recording.

Note 3: A recording may have been made ca. 1909 with Eva Turner,† but the   † spurious
         matrix number has not been traced; acc. to SHM (Le Grand Baton,
         Vol. 3 No. 2) the matrix may exist in HMV's vaults.

Note 4: Reverse side not Beecham.
Note 5: Speed 76 RPM. Label lists Beecham as conductor on A-7 and A-9; A-8 not
         seen.

Part 3 - Columbia Graphophone Company, 1915-1917

A-10   MOZART: The Magic Flute: Overture (2ss)

6559/60	Col. L-1001	Col. 65019-D
		Col. 7094-M
	in HMV ALP-1870/1 in Ang. 3621B	

A-11   BORODIN: Prince Igor: Polovtsian Dances (Abridged-2ss)

6561/2	Col. L-1002	Col. A-5808

A-12   (a) MASSENET: Manon: Minuet (1ss)
         (b) STRAUSS: Der Rosenkavalier: Act 2 Waltzes (1ss)

(a) 6563	Col. L-1020
(b) 6564	

A-13   (a) BORODIN: Prince Igor: Polovtsi March (1ss)^2
         (b) RIMSKY-KORSAKOV: Symphony No. 2 "Antar" : Oriental March (1ss)

(a) 6601	Col. L-1011
(b) 6604	

A-14   TCHAIKOVSKY: Symphony No. 6 in B minor, Op. 74: Excerpts
         (a) 2nd movement (Abridged-1ss)
         (b) 3rd movement (Abridged-1ss)

(a) 6602	Col. L-1016	Col. 65020-D
(b) 6603		Col. 7095-M

A-15   STRAVINSKY: The Firebird: Suite (Excerpts) 1910 Version
         (a) Dance of the Firebird (Abridged) and Scherzo (1ss)
         (b) Infernal Dance (1ss)

(a) 6797	Col. L-1040
(b) 6799	

A-16   (a) MENDELSSOHN: Midsummer Night's Dream: Scherzo (1ss)
         (b) ROSSINI: Barber of Seville: Overture (Abridged-1ss)

(a) 6800	Col. L-1075
(b) 6905	

A-17   (a) MOZART: Divertimento No. 2 in D, K. 131: Minuet No. 2 (1ss)
         (b) GRIEG: Symphonic Dance, Op. 64 No. 2 (1ss)

(a) 6904	Col. L-1132
(b) 6920	

A-18   (a) BERLIOZ: Roman Carnival Overture, Op. 9 (Abridged-1ss)
         (b) BERLIOZ: The Damnation of Faust: Hungarian March (1ss)

(a) 6907	Col. L-1105
(b) 6924	

A-19   (a) MOZART: Marriage of Figaro: Overture (1ss)
         (b) SMETANA : The Bartered Bride: Overture (Abridged-1ss)

(a) 6908	Col. L-1115	Col. 65018-D
(b) 6919		Col. 7093-M[Note 1]

A-20   (a) SIBELIUS: Kuolema, Op. 44: Valse Triste (1ss)
         (b) GOUNOD: Romeo and Juliet: Processional March (1ss)

(a) 6918	Col. L-1162
(b) 6921	

Note 1: On reverse of Scriabin: Poem of Ecstasy Side 5, cond. A. Coates.

Note 2: An American Columbia record exists of "Prince Igor-March of the Opera
         by Borodine" on A-6034, ₵ matrix 48739; whether or not this is a remastered
         copy of the Beecham recording is open to conjecture.

         ₵ A6034 not a Beecham recording

A-21   WEBER: Oberon: Overture (2ss)

           6922/3   Col. L-1104   Δ

A-22   GERMAN: Have you news of my boy, Jack?[1] (1ss)
           (Mme. Clara Butt, soprano)

           75414   Col. 7145

A-23   (a) BIZET: Fair Maid of Perth: Minuet (1ss)
       (b) LULLY: Les Amants Magnifiques: Minuet ($\frac{1}{2}$ ss)
       (c) MOZART: Marriage of Figaro: Sarabande ($\frac{1}{2}$ ss)

           (a) 76036   Col. L-1227
       (b)(c) 76037

A-24   DEBUSSY: Petite Suite (Arr. Büsser): Excerpts
       (a) En bateau (1ss)
       (b) Ballet (1ss)

           (a) 76225   Col. L-1248
           (b) 76226

                        END OF SECTION I

Additional information has been received concerning these recordings, in the form
of advertisements and reviews in The Sound Wave and Talking Machine Record,
which may tend to confirm or deny dates of recording listed herein; they are
indicated for whatever information they may reveal:

Vol. 6 No. 10 (Aug. 1912) P. 652: Review of A-7.
Vol. 6 No. 12 (Oct. 1912) P. 758: Advertisement by Odeon of A-9.
Vol. 7 No. 1 (Nov. 1912) P. 23: Advertisement by Odeon with photo of Beecham,
                                 listing A-8.
Vol. 9 No. 10 (Oct. 1915) P. 434: Reviews of A-10 and A-11.
Vol. 9 No. 12 (Dec. 1915) P. 528: Advertisement of A-13 with drawing of Beecham.
                                 Review of same on P. 543, same issue.
Vol. 10 No. 1 (Jan. 1916) Inside Front Cover full page advert. of Beecham's
                                 Columbia recordings with larger repro of drawing
                                 from previous issue. Page 41 lists A-14.
Vol. 10 No. 2 (Feb. 1916) P. 89: Review of A-14.
Vol. 10 No. 3 (Mar. 1916) P. 106: Advertisement photo of Beecham; on P. 107,
                                 advertisement of Beecham conducting
                     L.1013 Tristan und Isolde: Prelude & Liebestod
                     L.1021 Tannhäuser Grand March & Coriolan Overture.
                 (Ed. note: Contrary to the advert., these are not Beecham)
Vol. 10 No. 4 (Apr. 1916) P. 140: mention of Beecham's Russian music recordings,
                                 and of "Komarinskaya"[sic!] on Columbia 435, issued
                                 February 1914. (Ed. This was not Beecham)
Vol. 10 No. 6 (Jun. 1916) P. 239: Review of A-15.
Vol. 10 No. 11 (Nov.1916) P. 429: Advert. of Beecham Symphony in A-21 with repro of
                                 drawing from two earlier issues; also on P. 334
                                 listing of A-16.
Vol. 10 No. 12 (Dec. 1916) P. 481: Review of A-21.
Vol. 11 No. 1 (Jan. 1917) P. 34: Review of A-19.
Vol. 11 No. 3 (Mar. 1917) P. 105: Review of A-17.
Vol. 11 No. 5 (May 1917) P. 172: Review of A-20.
Vol. 12 No. 3 (Mar. 1918) P. 82: Review of A-23.
Vol. 13 No. 16 (Jun. 1919) P. 250/1: Advertisement of new Columbia recordings by
                                 Beecham and others. P. 261 review of A-24.
Vol. 16 No. 7 (Jul. 1922) P. 422: In an article on the horn referral is made to
----
  Note [1]Acc. to RS, this is a ballad type of patriotic song, specially composed
         by Edward German to words by Kipling for a Royal Philharmonic Society
         concert given by Beecham on Feb. 26, 1917 at about which time it may
         have been committed to wax.

  (continued from above)....."a good example of hand horn writing is afforded by
                     Mozart's Minuet No. 8 (Beecham Orchestra, Col. L.11327.."
                     (Ed. the number is unknown; may be A-17 to which he refers)

<u>SECTION II</u>

THE EARLY ELECTRICAL RECORDINGS FOR COLUMBIA GRAPHOPHONE COMPANY, ENGLAND, 1926-1932

A-25 ATTERBERG: Symphony No. 6 in C, Op. 31   (8ss)   △
          (Old Royal Philharmonic Orchestra)

     WAX 3962-5   Col. L-2160/3   Col. 7166/9-M
         3963-3   in Alb. 2[1]
         3964-3
         3965-1
         3966-3
         3967-3
         3968-5
         3969-1
          Recorded at Scala Theatre, 12 Aug 28

A-26 BEETHOVEN: Symphony No. 2 in D, Op. 36[2] (8ss)
          (London Symphony Orchestra)

     WRAX 2142-2 9 Nov 26   Col. L-1864/7   Col. 67223/6-D
          2143-2 9 Nov 26   in M-45
          2144-2 9 Nov 26
          2145-2 9 Nov 26
          2149-3 10 Nov 26
          2150-2 10 Nov 26
          2151-2 10 Nov 26
          2152-2 10 Nov 26
          Recorded at Scala Theatre

A-27 (a) BORODIN: Prince Igor: Polovtsian Dances[2] (3ss)   (London Symphony)
     (b) MENDELSSOHN: Midsummer Night's Dream: Scherzo[2] (1s)

     (a) WAX 1556-2 2 Jun 26   Col. L-1811/12   Col. 7138/9-M
             1557-2 2 Jun 26
             1558-3[3] 2 Jun 26
     (b) WAX 1393-1 31 Mar 26
          Place of recording unknown.

A-28 (a) BORODIN: Prince Igor: Polovtsi March[2] (1s)
     (b) RIMSKY-KORSAKOV: Symphony No. 2: Oriental March[2] (1s)
             (London Symphony orchestra)

     (a) WAX 3159-3 20 Dec 27   Col. L-2058   Col. 7193-M
     (b) WAX 3158-1 19 Dec 27
          Recorded at Fyvie Hall, London

A-29 DELIUS: Brigg Fair   (4ss)
          (London Symphony Orchestra)

     WAX 3887/90   11 Jul 28   Unpublished (4 takes of each side recorded)
          Recorded at Central Hall, Westminster

A-30 DELIUS: Brigg Fair   (4ss)   S H B 52   △
          (Unnamed orchestra)

     WAX 4335-5[4] 20 Nov 28   Col. L-2294/5   Col. 68154/5-D
         4441-2 11 Dec 28   in X-30
         4442-1 11 Dec 28
         4443-2 11 Dec 28
          Place of recording ~~unknown~~ Portman Rooms

A-31 DELIUS: Sea Drift   (7ss)
          (Dennis Noble, bar.; Manchester Opera Chorus; London Symphony Orchestra)

     WAX 4296/302   11 Nov 28   Unpublished (3 takes of sides 1 & 2 rec.,
     _____ Recorded at Portman Rooms   2 takes of sides 3 to 7 rec.)

[1]Columbia Modern Music Album Series.   [2]Recording Speed 80 RPM.
[3]WAX 1558-2 also issued.
[4]WAX 4335-10 also issued, 10 Jul 29. Probably London Symphony.

Early Electrical Recordings, 1926-1932

A- 32 DELIUS: Songs
      (a) La ciel est pas-dessus (1s)
      (b) Cradle Song (½s)
      (c) Irmelin Rose (1s)
      (d) The Nightingale (½s)
      (e) Evening Voices (1s)
        (Dora Labette, soprano; Sir Thomas Beecham, piano)

      (a) WAX 5105-?   10 Jul 29 (b)(d)(e) Col. L-2344 & Col. 9092-M
      (b) WAX 5069-1 24 Jun 29   (a)(c) Unpublished
      (c) WAX 5068-3 24 Jun 29 (b)(d)(e) HMV HLM-7033
      (d) WAX 5069-1 24 Jun 29
      (e) WAX 5104-2 10 Jul 29

    Place of recording unknown; possibly Portman Rooms.

A-33 DELIUS: On Hearing the First Cuckoo in Spring (2ss)   **SHB32**   Δ
    (Old Royal Philharmonic Orchestra)

    WAX 3156-2   Col. L-2096   Col. 67475-D
       3157-1   in X-31
    Rec. 19 Dec 27 at Fyvie Hall, London

A-34 DELIUS: Summer Night on a River (2ss)
    (Old Royal Philharmonic Orchestra)

    WA 7621-2   Col. D-1638   Col. 17017-D
      7622-1
    Rec. 12 Jul 28 in Central Hall, Westminster

A-35 DELIUS: A Village Romeo and Juliet: Walk to the Paradise Garden (2ss)
    (Old Royal Philharmonic Orchestra)   **SHB 32**   Δ

    WAX 3155-3   Col. L-2087   Col. 67474-D
       3160-1   in X-31
    Rec. 20 Dec 27 at Fyvie Hall, London

A-36 GOUNOD: Faust (Sung in English) (30ss)
    (M. Licette, H. Nash, R. Easton, D. Vane, H. Williams, M. Brunskill,
    R. Carr, BBC Chorus and Unnamed Orchestra)

    WAX 4843   10 Apr 29   Col. DX 88/103
        4816-2   3 Apr 29
        4827-2   8 Apr 29   (Excerpts) HMV HLM-7052:
        4817-2   3 Apr 29   WAX 4816, 4827 (DX 88, 89)
        5334-2 13 Jan 30   WAX 4821, 4822 (DX 92, 93)
        4818   4 Apr 29   WAX 5338, 5339 (DX 94)
        4841   9 Apr 29   WAX 4823, 4824 (DX 95)
        4819   4 Apr 29   WAX 4833, 4837, 5340 (DX 97, 98)
        4820-2   4 Apr 29   WAX 5336, 5337, 4842 (DX 102/103)
        4821-2   5 Apr 29
        4822   5 Apr 29
        4844   10 Apr 29
        5338-2 14 Jan 30[1]
        5339-2 14 Jan 30[1]
        4823-2   5 Apr 29
        4824   5 Apr 29
        4828-2   8 Apr 29
        4832-2   8 Apr 29
        4833-2   8 Apr 29
        4837   9 Apr 29
        4838-2   9 Apr 29
        5340-2 14 Jan 30[1]
        4829   8 Apr 29
        5335   13 Jan 30
        4830   6 Apr 29
        4845-1 10 Apr 29
        4839-5 14 Jan 30[1]
        4840-2   9 Apr 29
        4831   6 Apr 29   ---------------------------------------
        5336-2 13 Jan 30   [1]Conducted by Clarence Raybould. Entire work
        5337-3 13 Jan 30   recorded in Central Hall, Westminster.
        4842-2   9 Apr 29

Early Electrical Recordings, 1926-1932

A-37 HANDEL: Messiah (36ss)[1]
         (D. Labette, M. Brunskill, H. Eisdell, N. Walker, H. Williams,
         BBC Chorus, Unnamed orchestra)

WAX 2959-1	9 Jul 27	Col. 9320/37	Col. 68600/17-D
3093-2	8 Oct 27	Col. L-2018/35	in M-271 (2 Vol.)
2958-1	9 Jul 27		
2890-6	27 Jun 27	(Ss.2,3,15,16,19,	S.1 Overture only:
2933-4	1 Jul 27	20,22,23,27,28,	Col. 50092-D; 7189-M
2938-4	2 Jul 27	29,31,32,33,35	
2893-3	24 Jun 27	and 36):	Ss. 21 & 35 only:
2928-2	30 Jun 27	Col. DX-630/7	Col. 50093-D; 7190-M
2927-2	30 Jun 27		
2934-2	1 Jul 27		Ss. 3 & 17 only:
2937-4	1 Jul 27		Col. 50094-D; 7191-M
2981-4	Unknown		
2904-1	29 Jun 27		
2950-3	7 Jul 27		
2947-4	7 Jul 27		
2948-4	7 Jul 27		
2924-4	30 Jun 27		
2899-1	27 Jun 27		
2935-2	1 Jul 27		
2936-3	1 Jul 27		
2900-2	27 Jun 27		
2901-1	27 Jun 27		
2898-2	27 Jun 27		
2902-2	29 Jun 27		
2939-2	2 Jul 27		
2940-3	2 Jul 27		
2892-3	24 Jun 27		
2956-2	9 Jul 27		
2925-5	30 Jun 27		
2955-2	9 Jul 27		
2905-2	28 Jun 27		
2969-2	11 Jul 27		
2970-1	11 Jul 27		
3092-2	8 Oct 27		
2903-3	28 Jun 27		
2949-4	7 Jul 27		

A-38 (a) HANDEL: Messiah: Pastorale Symphony (1s)
         (b) HANDEL: Concerto Grosso No. 14: Larghetto & Polonaise (1s) (Unnamed Orch.)

      (a) WAX 2941-3 2 Jul 27   Col. L-2345   (a) Col. 71606-D
      (b) WAX 5106-2 10 Jul 29   (a) Col. 50092-D; 7189-M
         (a)Recorded in Central Hall, Westminster; (b) in Portman Rooms.

A-39 (a) MASCAGNI: Cavalleria Rusticana: Voi lo sapete (1s)
         (b) PUCCINI: Tosca: Vissi d'arte (1s)
         (Eva Turner, sop.; Unnamed orch.)

      (a) WAX 3930-2 18 Jul 28   Col. L-2118   (a) Col. 50109-D
      (b) WAX 3929-3 18 Jul 28   (b) Col. 50100-D
                                     HMV HQM-1209   Ang. COLC-114

         Rec. in Central Hall, Westminster.

A-40 MOZART: Divertimento No. 2 in D, K. 131: Minuet No. 2 (1s)
         (Old Royal Philharmonic Orchestra)

      WAX 4695-2 25 Feb 29   Col. 68646-D
      Place of recording unknown.   in X-42[2]

----

[1]Recorded in Central Hall, Westminster. Omits sections 13, 34-37, 39, 52-55 & 57.
Recording Speed 80 RPM. Sides 2 and 34 recorded in Portman Rooms.

[2]Remainder of this set not Beecham.

Early Electrical Recordings, 1926-1932

A-41 MOZART: Symphony No. 34 in C, K. 338 (6ss)
      (Old Royal Philharmonic Orchestra)

    WAX 4197-2 25 Oct 28   Col. L-2220/22   Col. 67661/3-D
        4198-2 25 Oct 28   in M-123
        4200-1 25 Oct 28
        4201-2 25 Oct 28
        4202-1 25 Oct 28
        4199-4 24 Oct 28
      Recorded in Portman Rooms.

A-42 MOZART: Magic Flute: Overture[3] (2ss)
      (London Symphony Orchestra)

    WAX 1384-2   Col. L-1001R   Col. 7123-M
        1385-2
      Rec. 30 Mar 26; place unknown.

A-43 PONCHIELLI: La Gioconda: Suicidio! (1s)
      (Eva Turner, sop.; Unnamed Orch.)

    WAX 3928-2 18 Jul 28   Col. 50100-D
      Rec. in Central Hall,   HMV HQM-1209
      Westminster

A-44 STRAUSS: Don Quixote, Op. 35 (10ss)[1]
      (New York Philharmonic Orchestra; A. Wallenstein, cl; M. Pollain, vla.)

    CSHQ 71658-1 Published   Col. LX-186/90   Vic. 7589/93
           -2   in M-144
       71659-1 Published   Vic. L-11633/5S
           -2   in LM-144
       71660-1 Published(LP)
           -2
       71661-1
           -2 Published
       71663-1 Published
       71664-1 Published (LP)
       71665-1
           -2 Published
       71666-1
           -2 Published
       71667-1 Published (LP)
           -2
       71668-1 Published
       71669-1 Published
       71670-1 Published (LP)
       71671-1 Published
           -2
       71672-1
           -2 Published
       71673-1 Published (LP)
           -2

      Recorded 7 April 1932, Carnegie Hall, New York

A-45 VERDI: Aida: Ritorna Vincitor! (2ss)
      (Eva Turner, sop; Unnamed Orch.)
    WAX 3931-3, 32-2 19 Jul 28 Col. L-2150   Col. 50099-D
      Rec. Central Hall,   Col. 5132-M
      Westminster   HMV HQM-1209   Ang. COLC-114

A-46 VERDI: Il Trovatore: D'amor dull 'ali (1s)
      (Eva Turner, sop; Unnamed orch.)
    WAX 3933-1 19 Jul 28   Col. L-2156[2]
      Rec. Central Hall, Westminster HMV HQM-1209   Ang. COLC-114

----

[1] A continuous recording without pauses for side-breaks. The long-play edition was
recorded on separate equipment at the same time as the 78RPM masters, with the
equivalent of two 78RPM sides on each LP side, hence 5 sides shown for the LP
edition.

[2] Beecham not named on label. Reverse cond. Stanford Robinson.

[3] Recording speed 80 RPM.

             END OF EARLY ELECTRICAL LISTING

SUMMARY OF BEECHAM'S RECORDING SESSIONS WITH THE L.P.O., 1933-1940

This is by no means a complete listing of everything recorded at these sessions, however it can be used as a guide to determine the chronological sequence of the recordings as they were made.

1933

January 5th - A-76, 98
May 6th - A-105
May 15th - A-105
May 18th - A-76
September 28th - A-82

1934

January 19th - A-98
April 9th - A-61   April 22nd - A-61
June 24th - A-55, 107
July 13th - A-107
September 24th - A-104, 107
October 8th - A-87
Leeds Festival - A-56, 64, 65, 74, 75, 89, 115
October 20th - A-104, 107, 103
November 14th - A-61, 107
December 4th - A-61
December 11th - A-61

1935

Mar. 22nd - A-103
April 3rd - A-103, 121 , 69
April 11th - A-70
April 17th - A-103
April 25th - A-70
May 24th - A-70
July 16th - A-121
July 20th - A-70
August 23rd - A-101
October 4th - A-80
October 10th - A-68
November 25th - A-102
November 26th - A-110
December 9th - A-102
December 14th - A-114

1936

February 28th - A-52, 53, 121
March 14th - A-57
April 3rd - A-102
May - A-124
May 29th - A-120
June 19th - A-53, 100, 123
September 2nd - A-62
September 28th - A-62
October 3rd - A-47
October 6th - A-84, 99
November 2nd - A-62
November 27th - A-49, 126
December 18th - A-79

1937

February 4th - A-97
March 22nd - A-58
October 10th - A-111
October 12th - A-78, 109
October 13th - A-91, 125
October 23rd - A-111
November 1st - A-111, 122
November 30th - A-90
December 16th - A-48
December 23rd - A-51
December 30th - A-51

1938

January 6th - A-63
January 7th - A-63
January 31st - A-63
February 1st - A-48, 113
February 11th - A-66, 67
June 28th - A-122
July 18th - A-63, 122, 127
October 3rd - A-83, 125
October 4th - A-125
October 7th - A-91
October 8th - A-91
October 11th - A-91   November 9th - A-77, 94
November 14th - A-112
November 15th - A-112   November 21st - A-50
November 25th - A-93
December 15th - A-108
December 21st - A-94

1939

January 11th - A-94
January 18th - A-81, 94

February 13th - A-60, 81, 94
April 12th - A-54, 72
June 23rd - A-112
July 4th - A-81, 93
July 7th - A-72, 112   November 7th - A-93
November 27th - A-88, 117
November 28th - A-85, 116
November 30th - A-59, 106
December 7th - A-118
December 18th - A-119

1940

January 4th - A-71, 106
January 12th - A-86
March 19th - A-95, 96
March 21st - A-95
March 26th - A-92
March 29th - A-73
April 2nd - A-73

SECTION III

A. THE PREWAR RECORDINGS FOR E.M.I. (COLUMBIA AND GRAMOPHONE CO.), ENGLAND

Part 1: The London Philharmonic Recordings, 1933-1940

A-47 BEETHOVEN: Symphony No. 2 in D, Op. 36 (8ss)

    CAX 7852-1, 53-1, 54-2A,   Col. LX 586/9   Col. 68988/91-D
       55-2, 56-1A, 57-1A,   in M-302
       58-1, 59-2A
    Rec. 3 Oct 36

    Also published: CAX 7856-3

A-48 BERLIOZ: Excerpts from Damnation of Faust (4ss)   SHB 55   △
    (a) Dance of the Sylphs[1]
    (b) Minuet
    (c) Hungarian March

    (a) CAX 8082-4 1 Feb 38   Col. LX 702/3   Col. 69173/4-D
    (b) CAX 8142-1, 43-2 16 Dec 37   in X-94
    (c) CAX 8144-2A 16 Dec 37   (a) in HMV ALP 1870/1 & Ang. 3621B

A-49 BERLIOZ: Roman Carnival Overture, Op. 9 (2ss)   CDM7 64032-2 △

    CAX 7890-2, 91-2 27 Nov 36   Col. LX 570   Col. 68921-D
                                       Col. 71623-D
                                       in M-552

A-50 BERLIOZ: Les Troyens: Royal Hunt and Storm (2ss)

    CAX 8392-1,-2
               21 Nov 38   Unpublished
      8393-1,-2,-3

A-51 BERNERS: The Triumph of Neptune: Ballet Suite (4ss)   CDM7 63405-2 △
    (Robert Alva, baritone)

    CAX 8145-1 23 Dec 37   Col. LX 697/8   Col. 69142/3-D
    CAX 8148-1, 46-1, 47-1 30 Dec 37   in X-92

A-52 BIZET: L'Arlesienne Suite No. 1 (4ss)   SHB55 △

    CAX 7742-1, 43-2, 44-1, 45-1   Col. LX 541/2   Col. 68743/4-D
    Rec. 28 Feb 36   in X-69

A-53 BIZET: L'Arlesienne Suite No. 2: Excerpts (2ss)   SHB55 △
    (a) Minuet No. 2
    (b) Farandole

    (a) CAX 7805-2 19 Jun 36   Col. LX 614   Col. 68882-D
    (b) CAX 7747-1 28 Feb 36

    Also recorded 28 Feb 36, unpublished: unspec. excerpt of above on CAX 7746-1,-2

A-54 BIZET: Carmen: Orchestral Suite, Arr. Beecham (4ss)   SHB55 △

    CAX 8551-1, 52-1, 53-1, 54-1   Col. LX 823/4   Col. 69689/90-D
    Rec. 12 Apr 39   in X-144

A-55 BIZET: The Fair Maid of Perth: Orchestral Suite, Arr. Beecham (4ss) SHB55 △

    CAX 7192-2, 93-2, 94-1, 95-2   Col. LX 317/18   Col. 9085/6-M
    Rec. 24 Jun 34   in X-28

----

[1] Beecham can be heard remarking to the orchestra at the conclusion,
"Thank you very much, gentlemen; first rate!" I'm most grateful!"

LPO Recordings, 1933-1940

A-56 (a) **BORODIN**: Prince Igor: Polovtsian Dances (3ss)   SHB100   △
    (b) **MOZART**: Mass in C minor, K. 427: Qui Tollis (1s)
       (Leeds Festival Choir, sung in English)

    (a) CAX 7344-1, 45-3, 46-2   Col. LX 369/70   Col. 68384/5-D
    (b) CAX 7341-3   in X-54
       Rec. at Leeds Festival, Oct. 1934   in M-238
                   (a,exc.)in HMV ALP 1870/1 & Ang. 3621B

A-57 BRAHMS: Symphony No. 2 in D, Op. 73 (10ss)

    CAX 7757-1, 58-2, 59-1, 60-2A,   Col. LX 515/19   Col. 68620/5-D
       61-2, 62-1, 63-1, 64-1,   in M-265
       65-1, 66-1
       Rec. 14 Mar 36

A-58 (a) BRAHMS: Tragic Overture, Op. 81 (3ss)
    (b) MOZART: The Marriage of Figaro: Overture (1s)

    (a) CAX 7963-2, 64-2, 65-1   Col. LX 638/9   Col. 69057/8-D
    (b) CAX 7966-1A   in X-85
       Rec. 22 Mar 37   (b)Col. 71606-D
               (b) in HMV ALP 1870/1 & Ang. 3621B
               (b) in WRC SHB-20   & Turn. THS-65022/6

A-59 CHABRIER: Espana Rhapsodie (2ss)   CDM7 63401-2   SHB55   A

    CAX 8667-1, 68-3   30 Nov 39   Col. LX 880   Col. 71250-D

A-60 DEBUSSY: Prelude to the Afternoon of a Faun (2ss)   SHB55   △

    CAX 8394-3, 95-4 13 Feb 39   Col. LX 805   Col. 69600-D

A-61 DELIUS: Society Set, Volume I [1]   SHB32   △
    (a) Paris-The Song of a Great City (6ss)
    (b) Eventyr (4ss)
    (c) Koanga: Closing Scene (2ss)
    (d) Hassan: Entr'acte and Serenade (1s)
       (London Select Choir)

    (a) CAX 7120-2, 21-5, 22-1,   Col. SDX 1/7   Col. 11068/74-D
       23-2, 24-2, 25-1 9 Apr 34   in M-305
    (b) CAX 7356-2, 57-2, 58-2,   (c) in HMV SEL 1700 (45RPM)
       59-2   14 Nov 34
    (c) CAX 7375-2 4 Dec 34
       7376-5 11 Dec 34
    (d) CAX 7377-4 11 Dec 34

    Existing test pressings: CAX 7377-2 4 Dec 34
                    7121-3, -4 22 Apr 34

A-62 DELIUS: Society Set, Volume II [1]   SHB32   △
    (a) Sea Drift (7ss)
    (b) Over the Hills and Far Away (3ss)
    (c) In a Summer Garden (3ss)
    (d) Fennimore & Gerda: Intermezzo (1s)
       (London Select Choir; John Brownlee, baritone)

    (a) CAX 7772-2, 73-1A, 74-1A, 75-2,   Col. SDX 8/14   Col. 11030/6-D
       76-4A, 77-1,78-4 2 Nov 36   in M-290
    (b) CAX 7845-1A, 46-1A, 47-2A 28 Sep 36
    (c) CAX 7849-2A, 50-2, 51-1 2 Sep 36
    (d) CAX 7848-2   28 Sep 36

----

[1]Announced for possible reissue on World Record Club in 1975 or 1976.

LPO Recordings, 1933-1940

A-63   DELIUS: Society Set, Volume III[1]   SHB 32   △
       (a) Appalachia (10ss)
       (b) Hassan: Closing Scene (2ss) (w Jan van der Gucht. Royal Opera Chorus)
       (c) Irmelin: Prelude (1s)
       (d) Koanga: La Calinda (1s)   Recorded Abbey Road Studio.

       (a) CAX 8153-2, 54-3, 55-2 6 Jan 38   Col. SDX 15/21   Col. 11137/43-D
           8157-2, 58-1, 59-2,   in M-355
           60-2   7 Jan 38   (b)(d) in HMV SEL 1700 (45 RPM)
           8156-3   6 Jan 38
           8167-2, 68-2   31 Jan 38
       (b) CAX 8256-2A, 57-2 18 Jul 38
       (c) CAX 8161-3   18 Jul 38
       (d) CAX 8169-2A 31 Jan 38

       Existing test of "Florida Suite" version of La Calinda recorded on
       CAX 8162-1, however opera version recorded and released on CAX 8169-2A.

A-64   DELIUS: An Arabesque (3ss)
       (London Select Choir; Roy Henderson, tenor)

       Test Take TT 1837/9   Unpublished
          Rec. at Leeds Festival, 5 Oct 34

A-65   DELIUS: Songs of Sunset (8ss)
       (London Select Choir; Olga Haley, soprano and Roy Henderson, tenor)

       Test Take TT 1788/95   Unpublished
          Rec. at Leeds Festival, 8 Oct 34

A-66   DELIUS: A Mass of Life: Introduction to Part 3 (1s)   SHB 100   △
       CAX 8188-1,-2 11 Feb 38   Unpublished

A-67   (a) DELIUS: Two Songs from the Danish (1s)
           1. The Violet (Holstein) 2. Autumn (Jacobson)
       (b) DELIUS: Seven Songs from the Norwegian (2ss)
           3. Twilight Fancies   7. Sweet Wenevil
              (Both above with Lisa Perli, soprano)[2]

       (a) CAX 8190-2 11 Feb 38   Unpublished
       (b) CAX 8192-1, 91-1 11 Feb 38

A-68   DELIUS: Summer Night on a River (2ss)
       CA 15315-1, 16-1 10 Oct 35   Col. LB 44   Col. 17087-D
                          4

A-69   DVORAK: Legend, Op. 59, No. 2 (1ss) Excerpt
       CAX 7507-1 3 Apr 35   Unpublished

A-70   (a) DVORAK: Slavonic Rhapsody, Op. 45 No. 3 (3ss)
       (b) DVORAK: Legend, Op. 59, No. 3 (1s)
       (a) CAX 7502-4A 24 May 35   Col. LX 402/3   Col. 68386/7-D
           7503-3   11 Apr 35   in X-55
           7504-4   20 Jul 35   in M-239
       (b) CAX 7521-1A 25 Apr 35   (b)Col. 12902-D

A-71   FRANCK: Symphony in D minor (10ss)
       CAX 8692-2, 93-2, 94-2, 95-1,   Col. LX 904/8   Col. 71277/81-D
           96-1, 97-1, 98-1, 99-1,   in M-479
           8700-1, 701-2
           Rec. 4 Jan 40

----

[1]Announced for possible release on World Record Club in 1975 or 1976.

[2]Pseudonym for Dora Labette.

12

A-72 GRIEG: Peer Gynt Suite No. 1, Op. 46 (4ss)

    CAX 8545-1   12 Apr 39   Col. LX 838/9   Col. 70370/1-D
        8546-2   7 Jul 39   in X-180
        8547-1   12 Apr 39
        8550-1   12 Apr 39

A-73 HANDEL: The Faithful Shepherd: Suite, Arr. Beecham (6ss)

    CAX 8776-2, 79-1, 80-1,   Col. LX 915/17   Col. 71135/7-D
       81-2, 78-1, 77-2   in M-458
    Rec. 2 Apr 40

    Existing unissued take, Pt. 3, CAX 8775-1, Rec. 29 Mar 40

A-74 HANDEL: Israel in Egypt: Excerpts (2ss)
    (a) But as for His People
    (b) Moses and the Children of Israel
    (Leeds Festival Chorus)

    (a) CAX 7379-3   Col. LX 378   Col. 68412-D
    (b) CAX 7342-1
    Rec. at Leeds Festival, Oct. 1934

A-75 HANDEL: Israel in Egypt: The Lord is a Man of War (2ss)
       (Leeds Festival Chorus)

    CA 14769-1, 70-1   Col. LB 20   Col. 17044-D
    Rec. at Leeds Festival, Oct. 1934

A-76 HANDEL: The Origin of Design: Suite, Arr. Beecham (2ss)   SHB100   △

    CAX 6636-1T2 18 May 33   Col. LX 224   Col. 68156-D
      6638-1   5 Jan 33

    Existing unissued take, Pt. 1, CAX 6636-1, Rec. 5 Jan 33

A-77 HANDEL: The Gods Go A'Begging: Excerpts (2ss)
    (a) Introduction and Fugato
    (b) Dream and Bourrée

    (a) CAX 8389-1,-2   Unpublished
    (b) CAX 8390-1,-2 9 Nov 38

A-78 HANDEL: The Gods Go A'Begging: Excerpt (1s) Unspec.

    CAX 8078-1,-2 12 Oct 37   Unpublished[1]

A-79 HAYDN: Symphony No. 93 in D (6ss)

    CAX 7899-1, 900-1A, 901-1,   Col. LX 721/3   Col. 69266/8-D
      902-1, 903-1, 904-1   in M-336
    Rec. 18 Dec 36

A-80 HAYDN: Symphony No. 99 in E-flat (6ss)

    CAX 7602-2A, 03-2, 04-3,   Col. LX 505/7   Col. 68630/2-D
      05-2A, 06-2, 07-1   in M-264
    Rec. 4 Oct 35

A-81 HAYDN: Symphony No. 104 in D "London"   (6ss)

    CAX 8427-3 13 Feb 39   Col. LX 856/8   Col. 70073/5-D
      8428-1, 29-2, 30-1 18 Jan 39   in M-409
      8602-1, 03-1   4 Jul 39   _____ Col. ML-4771

----

[1]CAX 8066, 8080 and 8081 are also said to be Beecham recordings but no details are available.

LPO Recordings, 1933-1940

A-82   MENDELSSOHN: Concerto in E minor, Op. 64 (7ss)[1] (Joseph Szigeti, violin)

CAX 6932-2, 33-2, 34-1, 35-2,   Col. LX 262/5   Col. 68159/62S-D
    36-1, 37-1, 38-1   in M-190
    Rec. 28 Sep 33
                           HMV HLM-7016   Col. ML-2217
                                      in Col. M6X-31513

A-83   MENDELSSOHN: The Hebrides (Fingal's Cave): Overture (2ss)

CAX 8171-3A, 72-3A   3 Oct 38   Col. LX 747   Col. 69400-D
                                          Col. 71621-D
                                          in M-552

A-84   MENDELSSOHN: A Midsummer Night's Dream: Excerpts (2ss)
    (a) Nocturne
    (b) Wedding March

(a) CAX 7861-1A   Col. LX 574   Col. 68888-D
(b) CAX 7860-1A   6 Oct 36

A-85   MENDELSSOHN: Ruy Blas: Overture (2ss)

CAX 8663-1, 64-1   28 Nov 39   Col. LX 879   Col. 70352-D

A-86   MOZART: Concerto No. 12 in A Major, K. 414 (6ss)
    (Louis Kentner, piano)

CAX 8703-3, 04-2, 05-4,   Col. LX 894/6   Col. 71492/4-D
    06-3, 07-1, 08-2   12 Jan 40   in M-544
                      in WRC SHB-20

A-87   MOZART: Concerto No. 4 in D major, K. 218 (6ss)
    (Joseph Szigeti, violin)

CAX 7288-2, 89-1, 90-1,   Col. LX 386/8   Col. 68339/41-D
    91-1, 92-2, 93-2   8 Oct 34   in M-224
                  in Elect. CO53-01364   Col. ML-4533
                                      in Col. M6X-31513

A-88   MOZART: Don Giovanni: Overture (2ss)

CAX 8661-3, 62-1   27 Nov 39   Col. LX 893   Col. 70365-D
                                          Col. 71620-D
                                        in M-552
                    in WRC SHB-20   in Turn. THS-65022/6

A-89   MOZART: Mass in C minor, K. 427: Kyrie (2ss)
    (Leeds Festival Chorus; Dora Labette, soprano)

CA 14771-1, 72-1   Col. LB 19   Col. 17050-D
    Rec. at Leeds Festival, Oct. 1934

A-90   MOZART: Symphony No. 29 in A, K. 201 (6ss)

CAX 8122-1, 23-1, 24-2,   Col. LX 687/9   Col. 69213/5-D
    25-1, 26-2A, 27-1 30 Nov 37   in M-333
                      in WRC SHB-20   Col. ML-4781
                                    in Turn. THS-65022/6

----

[1] LX issue had Szigeti in Paganini Caprice No. 9 on reverse of LX 263.
American issue had Side 8 blank.

LPO Recordings , 1933-1940

A-91 (a) MOZART: Symphony No. 31 in A, K. 201 (5ss)
       (b) HANDEL: The Gods Go A'Begging: Minuet and Hornpipe (1s)

    (a) CAX 8330-1 8 Oct 38   Col. LX 754/6   Col. 69470/2-D
         8331-2 7 Oct 38   in M-360
         8332-1 11 Oct 38   (b)Col. 72637-D
         8333-1 7 Oct 38   (a) in WRC SHB-20 (a) in Turn. THS-65022/6
         8334-1 11 Oct 38
    (b) CAX 8086-2A 13 Oct 37

A-92 MOZART: Symphony No. 34 in C, K. 338 (6ss)

    CAX 8769-4, 70-2, 71-2,   Col. LX 920/2   Col. 71583/5-D
       72-2, 73-2, 74-1   in M-548
       Rec. 26 Mar 40   in WRC SHB-20   Col. ML-4781
                                      in Turn. THS-65022/6

A-93 (a) MOZART: Symphony No. 35 in D, K. 385 (5ss)
       (b) MOZART: Divertimento No. 2 in D, K. 131: Adagio (1s)[1]

    (a) CAX 8396-1 25 Nov 38   Col. LX 851/3S   Col. 69822/4S-D
        8609-1, 05-1, 04-1,   in M-399
        8610-1 4 Jul 39   (a,4thmvmt)in HMV ALP 1870/1 & Ang. 3621B
    (b) CAX 8611-1 7 Nov 39   (a) in WRC SHB-20 (a) Col. ML-4770
                                    (a) Turn. THS-65033/5 &
   Existing unissued takes: CAX 8397-1,S.2, r. 25 Nov 38   THS-65022/6
                    8400-1,S.5, rec. 25 Nov 38

A-94 MOZART: Symphony No. 36 in C, K. 425 (7ss)

    CAX 8405-4 11 Jan 39   Col. LX 797/800S Col. 69737/40S-D
       8406-4 13 Feb 39   in M-387
       8407-2 21 Dec 38   in WRC SHB-20   Col. ML-4770
       8408-4 13 Feb 39   in Turn. THS-65022/6
       8416-3 11 Jan 39
       8431-1 18 Jan 39
       8426-2 11 Jan 39

      Existing unissued takes: CAX 8391-1, S.5, Rec. 9 Nov 38
                     CAX 8417-1, S.7, Rec. 21 Dec 38

A-95 MOZART: Symphony No. 38 in D, K. 504 (6ss)

    CAX 8757-1, 58-1, 59-2 19 Mar 40   Col. LX 911/13   Col. 71369/71-D
       8766-1, 67-2, 68-2 21 Mar 40   in M-509
                      in WRC SHB-20 in Turn. THS-65022/6

A-96 MOZART: Symphony No. 39 in E-flat, K. 543 (6ss)

    CAX 8751-2, 52-1, 53-1,   Col. LX 927/9   Col. 71115/7-D
       54-4, 55-1, 56-1   in M-456
       Rec. 19 Mar 40   in WRC SHB-20 in Turn. THS-65022/6

A-97 MOZART: Symphony No. 40 in G, K. 550 (6ss)

    CAX 7926-2, 27-2A, 28-4,   Col. LX 656/8   Col. 69103/5-D
       29-3, 30-1A, 31-1   in M-316
       Rec. 4 Feb 37   in WRC SHB-20   Col. ML-4674
              (Minuet)in HMV ALP-1870/1 & Ang. 3621B
                                 in Turn. THS-65022/6

A-98 (a) MOZART: Symphony No. 41 in C, K. 551 (7ss)
       (b) HANDEL: The Gods Go A'Begging: Sarabande & Tambourine (1s)

    (a) CAX 7050-2, 51-1, 52-3, 53-2,   Col. LX 282/5   Col. 68199/202-D
          54-3, 55-2, 56-2 19 Jan 34   in M-194
    (b) CAX 6637-1 5 Jan 33   (b) Col. 68881-D[2]
                    (a) in WRC SHB-20 (a) in Turn. THS-65022/6

---

[1] Announced as LX-853, but never issued. Both English and American issues have final
side blank.

[2] Label of 68881-D erroneously attributes the Sarabande to "Origin of Design" Suite.

LPO Recordings , 1933-1940

A-99   NICOLAI: The Merry Wives of Windsor: Overture (2ss)

      CAX 7862-1, 63-1A   6 Oct 36   Col. LX 596   Col. 68938-D
                                                                 Col. 71622-D
                                                                 in M-552

A-100   OFFENBACH: The Tales of Hoffmann: Excerpts (2ss)   __SHB55__   4
    (a) Barcarolle
    (b) Entr'acte (Epilogue)
        Duet (Act 2- Giuletta & Hoffmann)
        Intermezzo - Act 1

    (a) CAX 7806-2 19 Jun 36   Col. LX 530   Col. 68692-D
    (b) CAX 7807-1 19 Jun 36

A-101   PROKOFIEFF: Concerto in D, Op. 19 (5ss)
    (Joseph Szigeti, violin)

      CAX 7583-2, 84-3, 85-2,   Col. LX 433/5[1] Col. 68402/4-D
          86-2, 87-2   in M-244
        Rec. 23 Aug 35   HMV HLM-7016   Col. ML-4533
                                            in Col. M6X-31513

A-102   (a) PUCCINI: La Boheme: Act IV (7ss)   △
    (b) PUCCINI: La Boheme: Act III: "Donde lieta usci" (1s)
        (Heddle Nash, tenor; John Brownlee, baritone; Stella Andreva, soprano;
        Lisa Perli, soprano[2]; Robert Easton, bass)

      (a) CAX 7684-1, 85-1 25 Nov 35   Col. LX 523/6   Col. 68771/4-D
          7686-3, 87-2, 88-1,   in M-274
              89-2, 90-2 9 Dec 35   HMV HQM-1234
      (b) CAX 7771-5 3 Apr 36

A-103   RESPIGHI: Rossiniana: Suite after Rossini (4ss)

      CAX 7317-4 22 Mar 35   Col. LX 391/2   Col. 68390/1-D
        7318-5A 3 Apr 35   in X-56
        7321-4 17 Apr 35   in M-240
        7322-4A 17 Apr 35

    Existing unissued takes: CAX 7319-1, 7320-1, Rec. 20 Oct 34[3]

A-104   ROSSINI: La Gazza Ladra: Overture (2ss)

      CAX 7272-4, 73-3 20 Oct 34   Col. LX 353   Col. 68301-D

    Existing unissued takes: CAX 7272-2 24 Sep 34
                                7272-3 20 Oct 34
                                7273-1 24 Sep 34

A-105   (a) ROSSINI: La Scala di Seta: Overture (1½ss)
    (b) HANDEL: Solomon: Entrance of the Queen of Sheba (3/4ss)

    (a) CAX 6836-1 6 May 33   Col. LX 255   Col. 9077-M
  (a)(b) CAX 6837-1 6 May 33
                               (b) in HMV ALP 1870/1 & Ang. 3621B
                               (b) in HMV MRS-5185

    Existing unissued take: CAX 6836-2 15 May 33

----

[1]Reverse of LX 435 contains Paganini Caprice played by Szigeti. Reverse of S.5 in American Columbia album is blank.

[2]A pseudonym for Dora Labette

[3]These were to have been sides 3 and 4, and the published sides 3 and 4 were to have been sides 5 and 6.

LPO Recordings, 1933-1940

A-106 (a) ROSSINI: Semiramide Overture (3ss)
      (b) GRETRY: Zemire et Azor: Air de Ballet (1s)   SHB 55   Δ

      (a) CAX 8669-1, 70-1, 71-1 30 Nov 39   Col. LX 884/5   Col. 71329/30-D
      (b) CAX 8702-1 4 Jan 40   in X-215

A-107 (a) ROSSINI: William Tell: Overture (3ss)
      (b) HANDEL: The Gods Go A'Begging: Musette ($\frac{1}{2}$s)
          HANDEL: The Origin of Design: Minuet ($\frac{1}{2}$s)

      (a) CAX 7219-6, 20-4 24 Jun 34   Col. LX 339/40   Col. 68474/5-D
         7221-5 20 Oct 34   in X-60
      (b) CAX 7222-4 14 Nov 34   (b)Col. 68881-D

      Existing unissued takes: CAX 7219-1 13 Jul 34
                            7219-4,-5 24 Sep 34
                            7219-7 20 Oct 34
                            7220-1 13 Jul 34
                            7220-4 20 Oct 34
                            7221-1 13 Jul 34
                            7221-3,-4 24 Sep 34
                            7221-6 20 Oct 34

A-108 SCHUBERT: Symphony No. 5 in B-flat, D.485 (7ss)

      CAX 8409-1, 10-3, 11-1, 12-1,   Col. LX 785/8S   Col. 69576/9-D[1]
         13-1, 14-1, 15-1   in M-366
         Rec. 15 Dec 38   Col. ML-4771

A-109 SCHUBERT: Symphony No. 8 in B minor, D. 759 (6ss)

      CAX 8076-2A, 77-1A, 79-2,   Col. LX 666/8   Col. 69187/9-D
         73-2, 74-3, 75-1   in M-330
         Rec. 12 Oct 37

A-110 SIBELIUS: Society Set, Volume IV: Concerto in D minor, Op. 47 (8ss)
         (Jascha Heifetz, violin)

      2EA 2818-2, 19-1, 20-1, 21-2,   HMV DB 2791/4   Vic. 14016/9
         22-3, 23-3A, 24-3, 25-2A   in M-309
         Rec. 26 Nov 35   WRC SH-207   Vic. LCT-1113
                                                    Sera. 60221

A-111 SIBELIUS: Society Set, Volume V
      (a) Symphony No. 4 in A minor, Op. 63 (9ss)   CDM7 64027-2 Δ
      (b) The Return of Lemminkainen, Op. 22 No. 4 (2ss) CDM7 64027-2 Δ
      (c) The Tempest, Op. 109: Excerpts (3ss)
         (1) The Oak-Tree; Humoresque
         (2) Caliban's Song; Prospero; Miranda
         (3) Berceuse

      (a) 2EA 5820-4, 21-4, 22-4, 23-3,   HMV DB 3351/7   Vic. 12215/21
         33-4, 34-4, 35-4, 36-4,   in M-446
         56-3 Rec. 10 Oct 37 (a)(b) WRC SH-133
      (b) 2EA 5873-2, 74-1 23 Oct 37
      (c)(1) 2EA 5859-2 1 Nov 37
      (c)(2) 2EA 5857-1 1 Nov 37
      (c)(3) 2EA 5858-3 1 Nov 37

----

[1]Side 8 of American Columbia set not Beecham.

LPO Recordings, 1933-1940   △

A-112 SIBELIUS: Society Set, Volume VI
        (a) En Saga, Op. 9 (4ss)
        (b) In Memoriam, Op. 59 (2ss)
        (c) Pelleas and Melisande, Op. 46: Excerpts (3ss)
            (1) A spring in the park (½s)
            (2) Entr'acte (1s)
            (3) Death of Melisande (1½ss)
        (d) Kuolema, Op. 44: Valse Triste (1s)
        (e) The Tempest, Op. 109: Prelude (2ss)   **CDM7 644027-2**   △
        (f) The Bard, Op. 64 (2ss)

        (a) 2EA 6833-1, 34-1 14 Nov 38   HMV DB 3888/94   Vic. 12614/20
            7928-1, 29-1   7 Jul 39   in M-658
        (b) 2EA 6831-1, 32-1 14 Nov 38   (b)(f)WRC SH-133
        (c)(1)(3,Pt.1) 2EA 7930-1 7 Jul 39   (a)WRC SH-207
        (c)(3, Pt.2) 2EA 8006-2 23 Jun 39
        (c)(2) 2EA 7931-1   7 Jul 39
        (d) 2EA 6835-1 15 Nov 38
        (e) 2EA 6837-1, 38-1 15 Nov 38
        (f) 2EA 6840-1, 41-1 15 Nov 38

        Existing unissued takes: 2EA 6836-1, 6839-1, (a) Unid. exc. Rec. 15 Nov 38
                                  2EA 8009-1, 8010-2, (a) S. 3 & 4, Rec. 23 Jun 39
                                  2EA 8005-1, 8007-1,08-2, (c) Unid. exc. Rec.
                                      23 Jun 39

A-113 SIBELIUS: Finlandia, Op. 26 (2ss)   **CDM7 63397-2**   △

        CAX 8169-1, 70-2 1 Feb 38   Col. LX 704   Col. 69180-D

A-114 SIBELIUS: Four Historic Scenes, Op. 25: Festivo (2ss)

        CAX 7769-1, 70-1A 14 Dec 35   Col. LX 501   Col. 68590-D

A-115 SIBELIUS: The Tempest, Op. 109: Excerpts (2ss)
        (a) The Oak-Tree; Humoresque
        (b) Caliban's Song; Canon

        (a) CAX 7347-1   Col. 68409-D
        (b) CAX 7343-1
        Recorded at Leeds Festival, Oct. 1934

A-116 STRAUSS: Voices of Spring: Waltz, Op. 410 (2ss)

        CAX 8665-1, 66-1   28 Nov 39   Col. LX 867   Col. 70338-D

A-117 SUPPÉ: Morning, Noon and Night in Vienna (2ss)

        CAX 8659-1, 60-1   27 Nov 39   Col. LX 865   Col. 71439-D

A-118 TCHAIKOVSKY: Francesca da Rimini, Op. 32 (6ss)

        CAX 8676-1, 77-1, 78-1,   Col. LX 887/9   Col. 71036/8-D
            79-1, 80-3, 81-1   in M-447
        Rec. 7 Dec 39

A-119 TCHAIKOVSKY: Symphony No. 5 in E minor, Op. 65 (10ss)

        CAX 8690-1, 85-1, 91-1, 87-1, 88-1,   Col. LX 869/73   Col. 71194/8-D
            89-1, 86-3, 82-1, 83-1, 84-1   in M-470
        Rec. 18 Dec 39

LPO Recordings, 1933-1940

A-120 WAGNER: Die Götterdämmerung: Excerpts (4ss)   Δ
          (a) Act I: Hier sitz´ ich zur wacht (Ludwig Weber, bass)   RLS742
          (b) Act II: Hoi-ho! (Ludwig Weber, bass; Herbert Janssen, bar.,
                              and chorus)   SHB100

          (a) CAX 7906-1   Col. LX 636/7   Col. 69047/8-D
          (b) CAX 7907-1, 08-1, 09-1   in X-83
          Rec. at Covent Garden, 29 May 36

A-121 (a) WAGNER: A Faust Overture (3ss)
       (b) WAGNER: Lohengrin: Prelude to Act 3 (1s)

          (a) CAX 7508-2   28 Feb 36   Col. LX 481/2   Col. 68593/4-D
              7509-4   16 Jul 35   in X-63
              7510-4   28 Feb 36
          (b) CAX 7558-2   16 Jul 35

          Existing unissued takes: CAX 7508-1, -1A 3 Apr 35
                                    CAX 7509-2A 3 Apr 35
                                    CAX 7509-5 16 Jul 35

A-122 (a) WAGNER: Flying Dutchman: Overture (3ss)
       (b) WAGNER: Tannhäuser: Entry of the Guests (1s)

          (a) CAX 8101-2A, 02-2, 03-2A   Col. LX 732/3   Col. 69326/7-D
              Rec. 1 Nov 37   in X-107
          (b) CAX 8258-4A   18 Jul 38

          Existing unissued takes: CAX 8258-1A 28 Jun 38
                                    CAX 8258-3 18 Jul 38

A-123 WAGNER: Die Meistersinger: Prelude to Act I (2ss)

          CAX 7803-2A, 04-1A   19 Jun 36   Col. LX 557   Col. 68854-D

A-124 WAGNER: Die Meistersinger: Excerpts (4ss)   RLS742   Δ
          (a) Act I: Da zu dir der Heiland Kam (1s) (Covent Garden Chorus)
          (b) Act III:
              (1) Silentium....wach auf (1s) (Covent Garden Chorus)
              (2) Morgenlich Leuchtend (2ss) (Torsten Ralf, tenor; C.G. Chorus)

          (a) CAX 7910-1   Col. LX 645/6   Col. 69095/6-D
          (b)(1) CAX 7913-1   in X-87
          (b)(2) CAX 7914-1, 15-1
              Rec. at Covent Garden, May 1936 (a) in HMV ALP 1870/1 & Ang. 3621B

A-125 (a) WAGNER: Tannhäuser: Overture (Concert Version) (3ss)
       (b) BORODIN: Prince Igor: Polovtsi March (1s)

          (a) CAX 8083-2A, 84-5, 85-1 13 Oct 37 Col. LX 768/9   Col. 69413/4-D
          (b) CAX 8329-2   3 Oct 38   in X-123

          Existing unissued takes: CAX 8084-4 4 Oct 38

A-126 WEBER: Der Freischütz: Overture (2ss)

          CAX 7892-1A, 93-2A   27 Nov 36   Col. LX 601   Col. 68986-D

A-127 WEBER: Oberon: Overture (2ss)   SHB100   Δ

          CAX 8140-4A, 41-5   18 Jul 38   Col. LX 746   Col. 69410-D

                              END OF PART I

SECTION III

Part 2: Other recordings for Gramophone Co., 1937-40

A-128 BEECHAM, Adrian: Songs (Trad., words attrib. Shakespeare) (2ss)
         (a) Outward Bound (1s)
         (b) The Willow Song (½s)
         (c) Othello - O Mistress Mine (½s)
            (Nancy Evans, contralto; Sir Thomas Beecham, piano)

       (a) 2EA 8530-1   HMV C.3165
    (b)(c) 2EA 8531-1

       Recorded 15 Jan 40

A-129 MOZART: The Magic Flute, K. 620 (37ss)
            (Tiana Lemnitz, soprano; Erna Berger, soprano; Gerhard Hüsch,
            baritone; Wilhelm Strienz, bass; Helge Roswaenge, tenor;
            Irma Beilke, soprano; Heinrich Tessmer, tenor; Walter Grossman,
            bass; the Favre Chorus)

2RA 2448-5, 57-3, 25-3, 26-1,	HMV DB 3465/83S	Vic. 12551/9
20-3, 21-5, 59-5, 27-2,	DB 8475S/93	12560/9S
28-1, 17-2, 16-1, 32-2,		in M-541/2[1]
33-1, 34-1, 29-2, 18-2,		
36-2, 35-2, 56-2, 55-1,	HMV ALP-1273/5	Vic. LCT-6101
53-2, 58-3, 47-4, 39-1,	Elect 80471/3S	Turn. TV-4111/3
52-2, 19-1, 22-2, 51-3,	WRC SH-158/60	
37-2, 38-1, 49-1, 50-1,		
54-1, 30-1, 31-1, 23-2,	Aria: Papagena, Papagena	
24-1	in HMV ALP 1870/1 & Ang. 3621B	

       Recorded in Berlin, 1937

----

[1]Original issue side 38 blank; post-war American reissue fill-up was
 Mozart Serenade No. 13: Finale-Rondo from DB 6205 and 11-9809B.

SECTION III

B. THE NEW YORK PHILHARMONIC ORCHESTRA RECORDINGS (COLUMBIA, USA), 1942[1]

A-130   MENDELSSOHN: Symphony No. 4 in A, "Italian" (8ss)

    xco 32953/60   Col. 11956/9-D
    Rec. 15 Jun 42   in M-538

A-131   RIMSKY-KORSAKOV: Suite from "Le Coq d'Or" (4ss)

    xco 32919/22   Unpublished
    Rec. 13 Jun 42

A-132   (a) SIBELIUS: Symphony No. 7 in C, Op. 105 (5ss)
       (b) SIBELIUS: Pelleas and Melisande, Op. 46: Melisande (1s)

    (a) xco 32946   13 Jun 42   Col. 11890/2-D
           32947   15 Jun 42   in M-524
           32948   15 Jun 42   (b) Col. 12902-D
           32949   15 Jun 42   (a) Col. ML-4086
           32950   13 Jun 42   (b) Col. BM-13
    (b) xco 32961   15 Jun 42

A-133   TCHAIKOVSKY: Capriccio Italien, Op. 45 (4ss)

    xco 32942/5   Col. 11875/6-D
    Rec. 13 Jun 42   in X-229

----

[1]Beecham sued Columbia for removal of these recordings from circulation, claiming
he had not approved their issue. Apparently he lost.

SUMMARY OF BEECHAM'S RECORDING SESSIONS WITH THE L.P.O. AND R.P.O., 1944-1952

This is not a complete list of everything recorded at these sessions, however it is likely fairly complete and can be used as a guide to determine the chronological sequence of the recordings. Test pressings and unpublished recordings are included in the list, including the supplemental added takes at the end of the section.

<u>1944</u>

5 Dec - A-144
18 Dec - A-144, 153

<u>1945</u>

18 Jan - A-150
18/19 Jan - A-142
19 Jan - A-136
15/17 Aug - A-134
17 Aug - A-145
20 Aug - A-137, 145
24 Aug - A-135, 137, 143
3 Oct - A-138, 142
16 Oct - A-139, 140, 141
17 Oct - A-141, 154, 156
23 Oct - A-134, 135, 145, 146, 151
24 Oct - A-143, 146, 151, 155
27 Oct - A-143
28 Nov - A-153
5 Dec - A-143, 145, 152, 155
13 Dec - A-157, 158, 159
18 Dec - A-153
27 Dec - A-142, 143, 147, 148, 149, 152

<u>1946</u>

3 Oct - A-168
30 Oct - A-169, 174, 177, 178
1 Nov - A-168
6 Nov - A-164, 171, 233
22 Nov - A-183
25 Nov - A-166, 222
26 Nov - A-167, 179
28 Nov - A-203
30 Nov - A-184
2 Dec - A-219, 233
4 Dec - A-170
16 Dec - A-170, 233
18 Dec - A-218
19 Dec - A-170, 178, 181, 203, 233
21 Dec - A-168, 220
23/24 Dec - A-220

<u>1947</u>

3 Feb - A-193, 223
5 Feb - A-200, 215, 223, 237
8 Feb - A-233, 237
8/9 Feb - A-187, 220
9 Feb - A-199, 234
23 Feb - A-194, 217, 225
21 Mar - A-194, 195
24 Mar - A-225
26 Mar - A-194
29 Mar - A-200, 215, 223, 225
31 Mar - A-194
1 Apr - A-194, 220, 235
8 Apr - A-235
10 Apr - A-194, 195
11 Apr - A-199, 223, 229, 235
12 Apr - A-194
14 Apr - A-160, 166
15 Apr - A-194
16 Apr - A-152
18 Apr - A-194, 219, 235
22 Apr - A-166, 219
5 May - A-194
6 May - A-194
12 May - A-160, 203, 235
27 May - A-221
4 Jun - A-194
17 Jun - A-194
18 Jun - A-194
19 Jun - A-194
3 Jul - A-194
7 Jul - A-200, 212, 217

<u>1947</u>

8 Jul - A-194, 221
9 Jul - A-194
11 Jul - A-207
12 Jul - A-207, 211
10 Sep - A- 165, 221
11 Sep - A-205
15 Sep - A-187, 198
19 Sep - A-232
22 Sep - A-199, 238
27 Sep - A-195
29 Sep - A-236
30 Sep - A-163
4 Oct - A-226
7 Oct - A-226
8 Oct - A-226
13 Oct - A-224, 231
14 Oct - A-224
15 Oct - A-194, 199, 224, 227
27 Oct - A-228
28 Oct - A-228, 239
29 Oct - A-228, 230
5 Nov - A-225
5&6 Nov - A-200, 213, 225
6 Nov - A-187, 204
10 Nov - A-209
11 Nov - A-165, 221
21 Nov - A-230
25&26 Nov - A-189
26 Nov - A-189
27 Nov - A-189, 205
28 Nov - A-230
28/30 Nov - A-210
29 Nov - A-187, 189
1 Dec - A-189
8 Dec - A-205, 213
14 Dec - A-162, 230
15 Dec - A-162

<u>1948</u>

4 Jan - A-210, 213
5 Jan - A-189
6 Jan - A-189
7 Jan - A-189
8 Jan- A-189
10 Jan-A-189
16 Jan - A-236
20 Mar - A-226
18 Apr - A-189
20 Apr - A-196, 225
1 May - A-185
3 May - A-185
4 May - A-172, 185
6 May - A-185
7 May - A-185
8 May - A-172, 175, 178
30 Jun - A-189
3 Jul A-185
20 Jul - A-185

<u>1949</u>

14 Feb - A-176
18 Feb - A-172, 182
6 Apr - A-182
4 May - A-208
8 Jun - A-201
10 Jun- A-201, 206
11 Jun - A-197
20 Jun - A-161
23 Jun - A-191, 197
27 Jun - A-161, 191, 193, 214
28 Jun - A-192
1 Oct - A-180

<u>1950</u>

4 Jan - A-202
27 Jan - A-197

<u>1951</u>

16 Mar - A-191
3 Apr - A-186, 190

<u>1952</u>

29 Oct - A-173

SECTION IV

THE POSTWAR RECORDINGS FOR DECCA RECORDS LTD. & E.M.I. (GRAMOPHONE CO.), 1944-1952

Part 1: The London Philharmonic Recordings, 1944-1945[1]

A-134 BEETHOVEN: Symphony No. 4 in B-flat, Op. 60 (8ss)

2EA 9024-1	15/17 Aug 45	HMV DB 6280/3	Vic. 11-9349/52
9025-1	15/17 Aug 45		in M-1081
9027-1	15/17 Aug 45		Vic. LM-1026
9028-1	23 Oct 45		
9029-1	15/17 Aug 45		
9026-1	23 Oct 45		
9030-1	15/17 Aug 45		
9031-1	15/17 Aug 45		

Rec. Kingsway Hall

A-135 BERLIOZ: Les Troyens: Royal Hunt and Storm (2ss) △

2EA 9042-3	23 Oct 45	HMV DB 6241	Vic. 11-9667B,
9043-1	24 Aug 45	HMV ED 417	11-9668A
			in M-1141

Rec. Kingsway Hall

A-136 BERLIOZ: Les Troyens: Marche Troyenne (1s)

2EA 10390-1 19 Jan 45   Unpublished (approved)

A-137 (a) BORODIN: Prince Igor: Overture (3ss)
      (b) BERLIOZ: Les Troyens: Marche Troyenne (1s)

(a) 2EA 9039-1	20 Aug 45	HMV DB 6237/8	Vic. 11-9666,
9040-1	24 Aug 45		11-9667A,
9041-1	24 Aug 45		11-9668B
(b) 2EA 9044-1	24 Aug 45		in M-1141

Rec. Kingsway Hall

A-138 DELIUS: Concerto for Piano and Orchestra (5ss)
      (Betty Humby, piano)

2EA 10609-1,-2   Unpublished (rejected-masters destroyed)
    10610-1,-2,-3
    10611-1,-2   Rec. 3 Oct 45
    10612-1,-2
    10613-1,-2

A-139 DELIUS: Dance Rhapsody No. 2 (2ss)

2EA 10704-1,-2 Rec. 16 Oct 45   Unpublished
    10705-1

A-140 DELIUS: North Country Sketches (4ss-incomplete)

(#1 Part 1) 2EA 10707-1,-2   Unpublished
(#1 Part 2)   10708-1
(#2   )   10703-1,-2
(#4 Part 1)   10706-1,-2
        Rec. 16 Oct 45

A-141 DELIUS: A Song Before Sunrise (1s)

2EA 10702-1,-2 16 Oct 45   Unpublished

----

[1]Recorded in Studio No.1, Abbey Road, unless otherwise indicated.

LPO Recordings, 1944-1945

A-142 HANDEL: Concerto for Piano and Orchestra (Arr. Beecham) (5ss)
       (Betty Humby, piano)

     2EA 10385-1,-2   10388-1,-2,-3   Unpublished (Approved)
         10386-1,-2   10389-1
         10387-1,-2
          Rec. 18/19 Jan 45

     (Romanza only)
     2EA 10614-1   3 Oct 45
         10614-2,-3 27 Dec 45

A-143 HANDEL: The Great Elopement[1] (Arr. Beecham) (6ss)

     2EA 9045-1 24 Aug 45   HMV DB 6295/7   Vic. 11-9424/6
        10653-5 27 Dec 45   in M-1093
        10654-1,55-1 27 Oct 45
        10659-3   5 Dec 45
        10656-2   5 Dec 45

          Ss. 1,3,4 rec. Kingsway Hall

A-144 HAYDN: Symphony No. 97 in C (6ss)

     2EA 10331-1, 32-1 5 Dec 44   HMV DB 6222/4   Vic. 11-9204/6
        10333-3 18 Dec 44   DB 9001/3   in M-1059
        10334-1, 35-1, 36-2 5 Dec 44

A-145 MENDELSSOHN: Symphony No. 5 in D "Reformation" (7ss)

     2EA 9032-4 5 Dec 45   HMV DB 6316/9S   Vic. 11-9467/70
        9033-1, 34-1, 35-1,   in M-1104[2]
        36-1, 37-1, 38-1 20 Aug 45

         All exc. S. 1 rec. Kingsway Hall

A-146 MOZART: Abduction from the Seraglio: Overture (2ss)

     2EA 10658-1 23 Oct 45   HMV DB 6251   Vic. 11-9191
        10661-1 24 Oct 45

         Rec. Kingsway Hall

A-147 MOZART: La Clemenza di Tito (Titus): Overture (1s)

     2EA 10818-1   27 Dec 45   Vic. 11-9470
                                       in M-1104

A-148 MOZART: Cosi fan Tutte: Overture (1s)

     2EA 10815-1,-2 27 Dec 45   Unpublished

A-149 MOZART: The Impresario (Schauspieldirektor): Overture (1s)

     2EA 10814-1,-2,-3 27 Dec 45   Unpublished

A-150 MOZART: Serenade No. 13 "Eine Kleine Nachtmusik" (4ss)

     2EA 10381-2, 82-2, 83-2, 84-2   HMV DB 6204/5   Vic. 11-9809/9
         Rec. 18 Jan 45   HMV ED 419/20   in M-1163

                            (S.4,Rondo)...Vic. 11-8898
                                      in M-1014
        (S.4,Rondo,in postwar reissue of M-542, side 38)

A-151 RIMSKY-KORSAKOV: May Night: Overture (2ss)

     2EA 10657-1 23 Oct 45   Unpublished
        10660-1,-2 24 Oct 45

         Rec. Kingsway Hall

A-152 RIMSKY-KORSAKOV: May Night: Overture (2ss)

     2EA 10789-3 27 Dec 45   HMV DB 6308
----------- 10790-1   5 Dec 45 ----

[1]Suite No. 1: The Pump Room, The Linleys, The Hunting Dance, Love Scene, the Weary
  Flunkies, The Plot, Sarabande, Hornpipe, Beau Nash, 2nd Love Scene, Intermezzo, Jig.

[2]Final side in American Victor set: Clemenza di Tito Overture, see below.

LPO Recordings, 1944-1945; BBC Symphony Recordings, 1945

A-153 SCHUBERT: Symphony No. 6 in C, D.589   (7ss)

    2EA 10318-4 28 Nov 45   HMV DB 6200/3S   Vic. 11-8895/8
        10319-4 28 Nov 45   DB 8977S/80   in M-1014[1]
        10320-5, 23-4, 24-3,   DB 11153/6S
           29-3, 30-4   18 Dec 44

A-154 STRAUSS: Salome: Dance of the Seven Veils (Part 2 only) (1s)

    2EA 10652-1   17 Oct 45   Unpublished (Rejected-not repeated)

    Rec. Kingsway Hall

A-155 TCHAIKOVSKY: Eugene Onegin: Op. 24: Excerpts (2ss)   Δ
      (a) Polonaise
      (b) Waltz

      (a) 2EA 10788-1 5 Dec 45   <u>HMV DB 6266</u>   Vic. 11-9421
      (b) 2EA 10662-1 24 Oct 45

      (b) Rec. Kingsway Hall

A-156 WAGNER: Das Rheingold: Entrance of the Gods into Valhalla (2ss)
      (P. Jones, G. Hancock, T. Barry, N. Evans, G. Ripley)

    2EA 9050-1,-2,-3   Unpublished – rejected, not repeated
        10651-1,-2

    Rec. 17 Oct 45, Kingsway Hall

END OF LPO LISTING

Part 2: <u>The BBC Symphony Recordings, 1945</u> [2]

A-157 MASSENET: Manon: Prelude to Act 3 (1s)

    2EA 10791 (?)   Unpublished (rejected)

    Rec. 13 Dec 45

A-158 REZNICEK: Donna Diana: Overture (1s)

    2EA 10792 (?)   Unpublished (rejected)

    Rec. 13 Dec 45

A-159 SIBELIUS: Karelia, Op. 11: Excerpts (2ss)
      (a) Intermezzo
      (b) Alla marcia   <u>CDM7 63397-2</u>   Δ

      (a) 2EA 10794-1   HMV DB 6248   Vic. 11-9568 Δ
      (b) 2EA 10793-1

    Rec. 13 Dec 45

END OF BBC SYMPHONY LISTING

----

[1] Final side in American Victor album: Rondo from Serenade No. 13, see above.

[2] Rec. Abbey Road Studio #1; matrix numbers for unpublished items are conjectural.

<u>SECTION IV</u>

THE POSTWAR RECORDINGS FOR DECCA RECORD CO. & EMI (GRAMOPHONE CO.), 1944-1952

Part 3: <u>The Royal Philharmonic Orchestra Recordings</u>[1]
<u>1946-1952</u>

A-160 (a) BACH: Christmas Oratorio: Sinfonia (1½ss)
     (b) HANDEL: Amaryllis Suite: Gavotte (½s)

    (a) 2EA 11842-3
  (a)(b) 2EA 11843-4 Rec. 12 May 47
                                         Vic. 12-0583

A-161 BANTOCK: Fifine at the Fair (8ss)   CDM7 63405-2   △
     (Jack Brymer, clarinet; Albert Cayzer, viola)

      2EA 14013-5A, 14-1, 15-1, 16-1A   HMV DB 21145/8
         Rec. 20 Jun 49   DB 9557/60
        14035-2, 36-2, 37-1, 38-1   HMV BLP-1016   Vic. LHMV-1026
         Rec. 27 Jun 49   HMV HQM-1165[2]

A-162 BAX: The Garden of Fand (4ss)   CDM7 63405-2   △

      2EA 12635-1 14 Dec 47   HMV DB 6654/5
         12632-2 14 Dec 47(?)   HMV HQM-1165
         12640-2, 41-2 15 Dec 47

A-163 BEETHOVEN: Concerto No. 4 in G, Op. 58 (8ss)   SHB100   △
     (Artur Rubinstein, piano)

      2EA 12331-2, 32-1, 33-3, 34-1,   HMV DB 6732/5   Vic. M-1345
         35-2, 36-2, 37-1, 38-1   DB 9405/8

        Rec. 30 Sep 47   Vic. LCT-1032

A-164 BERLIOZ: Le Corsaire: Overture, Op. 21 (2ss)

      2EA 11382-1, 83-1 6 Nov 46   HMV DB 6357   Vic. 11-9955

A-165 BERLIOZ: King Lear Overture, Op. 4 (4ss)   CDM7 64032-2 △

      2EA 10680-5 11 Nov 47   HMV DB 6581/2
         10681-2, 82-2 10 Sep 47   DB 9614/5
         10683-1 11 Nov 47

        Rec. Kingsway Hall

A-166 DEBUSSY: Printemps (4ss)   SHB100   △

      2EA 11439-4 14 Apr 47   HMV DB 6549/50   Vic. 12-0809/10
         11440-5 22 Apr 47   in M-1293
         11441-2, 42-1 25 Nov 46   Vic. LM-9001

A-167 DELIUS: Brigg Fair (4ss)   SHB 34   △

      2EA 11443-1, 44-1, 45-2, 46-1   HMV DB 6452/3   Vic. 12-1202/3
         Rec. 26 Nov 46   in M-1206
                                       Vic. 18-0108/9
                                       in V-14

----

[1] Recorded Abbey Road Studio No. 1 except as indicated. The rights for many of
these recordings have reverted to RCA Records through agreements made at the
time the company severed relations with HMV in the late 1950's. RCA have
indicated they intend to reissue their material, beginning with the complete
Faust in the fall of 1975.
[2] Sleeve note incorrectly states recording date of July, 1949.

RPO Recordings, 1946-1952

A-168 (a) DELIUS: Concerto for Violin and Orchestra (5ss)   SHB34   Δ
           (Jean Pougnet, violin)
       (b) DELIUS: Irmelin: Prelude (1s)   SHB34   Δ

       (a) 2EA 11329-3, 30-2, 31-1, 32-3, 33-1   HMV DB 6369/71
               Rec. 3 Oct & 1 Nov 46   DB 9092/4
       (b) 2EA 11530-1   21 Dec 46   (a)HMV ALP-1890
                                                 (b)HMV ALP-1889

A-169 DELIUS: Concerto for Piano & Orchestra (5ss)
           (Betty Humby, piano)

       2EA 11318-1,-1A,-2,-2A   Unpublished
           11319-1,-2
           11320-1,-2,
           11321-1,-2
           11322-1,-2

       Rec. 30 Oct 46

A-170 (a) DELIUS: Concerto for Piano & Orchestra (5ss)   SHB34   Δ
           (Betty Humby, piano)
       (b) DELIUS: Marche Caprice (1s)

       (a) 2EA 11318-3, 19-3 4 Dec 46   HMV DB 6428/30   Vic. 12-0028/30
           11320-5, 21-4 16 Dec 46   DB 9273/5   in M-1185
           11322-3 4 Dec 46   (a)HMV ALP-1890   (a)Vic. LVT-1045
       (b) 2EA 11521-2 19 Dec 46

A-171 DELIUS: Dance Rhapsody No. 1 (3ss)
       2EA 11371-1,-2   Unpublished
           11372-1,-2   6 Nov 46
           11373-1,-2
A-172 DELIUS: Dance Rhapsody No. 1 (2ss)

       2EA 13013-1,-2 4&8 May 48   Unpublished
           13013-3,-4 18 Feb 49
           13014-1,-2 4&8 May 48
           13014-3,-4 18 Feb 49
A-173 (a) DELIUS: Dance Rhapsody No. 1 (3ss)   SHB34   Δ
       (b) DELIUS: Hassan: Entr'acte and Serenade (1s)   SHB34   Δ

       (a) 2EA 16980-2A, 81-3A, 82-3A   HMV DB 9785/6
       (b) 2EA 16983-2A   HMV ALP-1889   Vic. LHMV-1050
               Rec. 29 Oct 52[1]   (a) HMV HQM-1165   Vic. LVT-1020
                                               (b) HMV ALP-1870/1 (b)Ang. 3621B

A-174 DELIUS: Dance Rhapsody No. 2 (2ss)   SHB34   Δ
       2EA 11234-1,-2   HMV DB-6451[2]
           11235-1,-2 3 Oct 46

A-175 DELIUS: A Mass of Life: Part 3: Prelude (1s)
       2EA 13033   8 May 48   2   Unpublished

A-176 DELIUS: North Country Sketches (6ss)
       2EA 13596-1,-2,-3   Unpublished
           13597-1,-2
           13598-1,-2
           13599-1,-2   Rec. 14 Feb 49
           13600-1,-2
           13601-1,-2
----
[1]Tape original - 78 RPM's are dubs.
[2]Assigned but apparently not issued. Rumored to have been in HMV's special order
   catalog for a short time.

RPO Recordings, 1946-1952

A-177 DELIUS: On Hearing the First Cockoo in Spring: Part 1 (1s)

    2EA 11327-1,-2 30 Oct 46   Unpublished

A-178 DELIUS: On Hearing the First Cuckoo in Spring (2ss)   SHB34   Λ

    2EA 13034-1 8 May 48   HMV DB 6923   Vic. 12-1093
         11328-3 19 Dec 46   (45RPM) HMV 7er 5198   Vic. LHMV-1050
                                             Vic. LVT-1020
                                           Vic. EHA-12 (45 RPM)

A-179 DELIUS: On the Mountains (3ss)

    2EA 11447-1,-2   Unpublished
       11448-1,-2   Rec. 26 Nov 46
       11449-1,-2

A-180 DELIUS: Two Songs from the Danish
        (a) The Violet   (b) Autumn
          (Elsie Suddaby, soprano)

      Tape master 539/40   Rec. 1 Oct 49   Unpublished
  (a) 2EA 14221-1,-2

A-181 DELIUS: A Song Before Sunrise (2ss)

    2EA 11522-1, 23-1 19 Dec 46   Unpublished

A-182 (a) DELIUS: A Song Before Sunrise (1½ss) ⎫
     (b) DELIUS: Summer Evening (2 half sides) ⎬   SHB34   Δ
     (c) DELIUS: Summer Night on the River (1½ss) ⎭

    (a) 2EA 13615-2   18 Feb 49   HMV DB 21021/2
         13745-1   6 Apr 49   DB 9757/8
    (b) 2EA 13614-2   18 Feb 49   (b) HMV ALP-1889 Vic. LHMV-1050
         13615-2   18 Feb 49   Vic. LVT-1020
    (c) 2EA 13613-1   18 Feb 49   (c)Vic. EHA-12 (45 RPM)
         13614-2   18 Feb 49

A-183 DELIUS: A Song of the High Hills (6ss)   SHB34   Δ
       (Luton Choral Society)

    2EA 11429-2, 30-2, 31-2,   HMV DB 6470/2   Vic. 12-0031/2,
        32-2, 33-2, 34-2   DB 9151/3   12-0033A,
                                            12-0034A
      Rec. 22 Nov 46   in M-1185
                         HMV ALP-1889   Vic. LVT-1045

A-184 DELIUS: Songs of Sunset (8ss)   SHB 34   Δ
      (Nancy Evans, Redvers Llewellyn, BBC Chorus)

    2EA 11462/9   Rec. 30 Nov 46   Unpublished

A-185 DELIUS: A Village Romeo and Juliet (24ss)   SHB34   Δ
      (Dennis Dowling, Margaret Ritchie, René Soames, Dorothy Bond,
     Lorely Dyer, Frederick Sharp, Gordon Clinton, RPO Chorus)

    2EA 13009-2 4 May 48   HMV DB 6751/62
       13010-4 3 Jul 48   DB 9306/17
       13027-4 3 Jul 48   Delius Fellowship, Vol. 1 & 2
       13011-2 4 May 48
       12990-2 1 May 48
       12991-2 1 May 48

    (Continued next page)

RPO Recordings, 1946-1952

A-185 DELIUS: A Village Romeo and Juliet (Continued from previous page)

2EA 12992-1	1 May 48	13022-4	20 Jul 48
12993-3	3 May 48	13021-1	6 May 48
12994-1	1 May 48	13007-3	3 Jul 48
12998-2	3 May 48	13012-1	4 May 48
12999-2	3 May 48	13023-2	6 May 48
13000-2	3 May 48	13024-2	7 May 48
13015-2	6 May 48	13025-2	7 May 48
13017-2	6 May 48	13059-3	20 Jul 48
13016-4	20 Jul 48	13026-1	7 May 48

A-186 DELIUS: When Twilight Fancies (1s)
           (Elsie Suddaby, soprano)

   2EA 15485-3 3 Apr 51

                              in HMV ALP-1870/1 &   Ang. 3621B
                                                     Vic. LHMV-1050
                                                     Vic. LVT-1020

A-187 DVORAK: The Golden Spinning Wheel, Op. 109 (6ss)   SHB100   △

   2EA 11646-3 29 Nov 47   HMV DB 6656/8   Vic. 12-0797/9
       11647-4 15 Sep 47   DB 9284/6   in M-1291
       12275-3, 76-2 15 Sep 47
       12277-2 6 Nov 47
       12278-1 15 Sep 47

A-188 EASDALE: The Red Shoes: Ballet Sequence (4ss)
                                                          Jp. Vic. ND-372/3
   RM 170/3   in JAS-93

   Recorded 1949 from film soundtrack

A-189 GOUNOD: Faust (32ss)
           (Géori-Boué, Georges Noré, Roger Rico, Roger Bourdin, Henrietta
            St. Arnaud, Ernest Frank, Betty Bannerman, RPO Chorus)

   2EA 12542-4 10 Jan 48   HMV DB 9422/37   Vic. 12-0821/8,
       12554-1 5 Jan 48   12-0837/44
       12558-2 5 Jan 48   ss.6,7,10,24, 22,23,   in M-1300/1
       12572-2 8 Jan 48   27 & 28) repressed on   in MC-124
       12573-4 30 Jun 48   HMV DB 6964/7
       12553-3 7 Jan 48   Vic. LCT-6100
       12545-1 25 & 26 Nov 47   (exc) Vic. LCT-1100
       12547-2 26 Nov 47
       12556-2 5 Jan 48
       12566-1 7 Jan 48
       12543-2 25 & 26 Nov 47
       12563-2 6 Jan 48
       12568-3 8 Jan 48
       12551-2 29 Nov 47
       12544-2 25 & 26 Nov 47
       12548-3 27 Nov 47
       12559-2 6 Jan 48
       12560-3 30 Jun 48
       12561-3 30 Jun 48
       12564-2 8 Jan 48
       12562-2 6 Jan 48
       12546-2 25 & 26 Nov 47
       12549-2 27 Nov 47
       12552-2 1 Dec 47
       12567-3 7 or 8 Jan 48
       12570-2 8 Jan 48
       12557-1 8 Jan 48
       12550-2 27 Nov 47
       12555-4 18 Apr 48
       12569-1 8 Jan 48
       12571-2 8 Jan 48
       12565-1 7 Jan 48

RPO Recordings, 1946-1952

A-190 HANDEL-BEECHAM: The Great Elopement: Suites 1 and 2 Excerpts (4ss)[1]

      2EA 15458-2, 86-2, 87-3, 88-1B   HMV DB 21396/7
         Rec. 3 Apr 51   DB 9672/3
                                      Vic. LHMV-1030

A-191 HANDEL-BEECHAM: The Great Elopement: Excerpts (1s each)
#1 & #5(March and Serenade) 2EA 15458-1 16 Mar 51   Unpublished
   #2(The Exquisitor)   2EA 14039-1,-2 27 Jun 49
#9 & #10(Minuet & Hornpipe) 2EA 13981-1,-2 23 Jun 49

A-192 HANDEL-BEECHAM: The Gods Go A'Begging (4ss)

      2EA 14043-1,-2   Unpublished
         14044-1,-2
         14045-1,-2 Rec. 28 Jun 49
         14046-1,-2

A-193 HANDEL: Amaryllis Suite: (a) Sarabande; (b) Scherzo

    (a) 2EA 14042-1,-2 27 Jun 49   Unpublished
    (b) 2EA 11019-1,-2   3 Feb 47

A-194 HANDEL: Messiah (42ss)[2]

      2EA 12433-2   15 Oct 47   (ss.1 & 13 only) HMV DB 6879   Vic. 12-0086/96,
          11664-2   23 Feb 47   12-0108/17
          11844-2   15 Apr 47   in M-1194/5
          11845-2   15 Apr 47   (ss.13 & 33) Vic. 12-0584
          11904-2   5 May 47   HMV ALP 1077/80   Vic. LCT-6401
          11740-3   9 Jul 47   (exc)Vic. LCT-1130
         11792-4   18 Jun 47
          11762-2   26 Mar 47
          11833-2   10 Apr 47   (Elsie Suddaby, soprano; Marjorie Thomas, con.;
          12140-5   15 Oct 47   Heddle Nash, tenor; Trevor Anthony, bass;
          11741-4   3 Jul 47   Luton Choral Society & special chorus)
          11841-2   12 Apr 47
          11665-2   23 Feb 47
          11839-1   12 Apr 47
          11811-3   17 Jun 47
          11809-1   1 Apr 47
          11810-4   17 Jun 47
          11791-2   31 Mar 47
          11730-2   21 Mar 47
          11763-1   26 Mar 47
          11764-1   26 Mar 47
          11905-2   5 May 47
          12141-1   19 Jun 47
          11906-1   5 May 47
          12139-2   18 Jun 47
          11846-2   15 Apr 47
          11853-2   3 Jul 47
          11913-2   6 May 47
          12166-2   9 Jul 47
          11832-4   19 Jun 47
          11798-4   8 Jul 47
          12081-2   4 Jun 47
          11840-2   12 Apr 47
          11850-2   18 Apr 47
          11851-4   17 Jun 47
          12153-2   8 Jul 47
          12154-1   9 Jul 47
          12082-2   4 Jun 47
          11852-4   3 Jul 47
          12142-2   19 Jun 47
          11914-2   6 May 47
          11915-4   8 Jul 47

-----------------------------------   [Suite No. 1: Minuet, the Quarrel, Hornpipe]
[1]Probably tape origin. Movements recorded [Suite No. 2: March, Serenade, Madrigal]
[2]Side 1 of the 78 RPM version includes a talk on the work by Beecham. Sections
   34 and 35 of the work are omitted. Talk also included start of side 1 on LP.

RPO Recordings, 1946-1952

A-195 HANDEL: Messiah: Excerpts (3ss)
    (a) Glory to God (with Chorus) (½s)
    (b) There were Shepherds (with Suddaby) (½s)
    (c) For unto us.... (with chorus) (1s)
    (d) Introductory talk by Beecham (1s)

    (a)(b) 2EA 11831-1 10 Apr 47   Unpublished
    (c)   2EA 11731-1,-2 21 Mar 47
    (d)   2EA 12262-1 27 Sep 47

A-196 HAYDN: Symphony No. 40 in F (4ss)   SHB100   Δ
    2EA 12935-1, 36-1, 37-2, 38-1   HMV DB 6823/4
      Rec. 20 Apr 48   (45RPM) HMV 7er 5093

A-197 HAYDN: Symphony No. 102 in B-flat (6ss)
    2EA 13975-2 11 Jun 49   HMV DB 21042/4
       13976-2 23 Jun 49   DB 9449/51
       13977-1, 78-2 11 Jun 49
       13979-3C 27 Jan 50
       13980-1 23 Jun 49

A-198 LISZT: Orpheus: Part 1 only (1s)
    2EA 12287-1 15 Sep 47   Unpublished- not repeated

A-199 (a) LISZT: Orpheus (3ss)
    (b) MASSENET: La Vierge: Last Sleep of the Virgin (1s) CDM 7 63401-2 Δ

    (a) 2EA 12312-3 15 Oct 47   HMV DB 6644/5 (a)Vic. 12-0817,
         12313-1,14-1 22 Sep 47   12-0818A,
    (b) 2EA 11648-3 11 Apr 47   in M-1295[1]
                              (b)Vic. 12-0688

A-200 MÉHUL: Les Deux Aveugles de Tolède: Overture (2ss)
    2EA 11630-1 5 Feb 47   HMV DB 21084   Vic. 12-0594
       11631-7 5 & 6 Nov 47   in M-1264

    Unpublished takes: Pt.2: 2EA 11631-1,-2 5 Feb 47
                      11631-3,-4 29 Mar 47
                      11631-5,-6 7 Jul 47
                      11631-8,-9 5 & 6 Nov 47

A-201 MENDELSSOHN: Concerto in E minor, Op. 64 (6ss)   SHB100 Δ
    (Jascha Heifetz, violin)

    2EA 13947-2T 10 Jun 49   HMV DB 6956/8   Vic. 12-1103/5
       13948-1 8 Jun 49   DB 9413/5   in M-1356
       13949-2 8 Jun 49   HMV FALP-136 Vic. LM-18
       13950-1 8 Jun 49   Vic. LM-9016
       13951-4A 10 Jun 49   Sera. 60162
       13952-1 10 Jun 49

A-202 MENDELSSOHN: Ruy Blas: Overture: Part 1 only (1s)
    2EA 13814-1A 4 Jan 50   Unpublished - not repeated

A-203 (a) MENDELSSOHN: A Midsummer Night's Dream: Overture (3ss)
    (b) HANDEL: Amaryllis Suite: Scherzo (1s)

    (a) 2EA 11452-2, 53-2 28 Nov 46   HMV DB 6820/1 (b)Vic. 12-0592A
         11454-3 19 Dec 46   in M-1264
      (b) 2EA 11619-3 12 May 47

---

[1]Final side of M-1295 is Chabrier: Marche Joyeuse from DB-6422; see Tchaikovsky: Romeo and Juliet Overture.

RPO Recordings, 1946-1952

A-204 MENDELSSOHN: Songs without words, Nos. 44 and 45[1] (1s)

    2EA 12508-1,-2,-3   6 Nov 47   Unpublished

A-205 (a) MENDELSSOHN: Fair Melusine Overture (3ss)
      (b) MENDELSSOHN: Scherzo from Symphony No. 1 in C^2 (1s)

    (a) 2EA 12268-1 11 Sep 47   HMV DB 6652/3   (b) Vic.12-0688
            12269-4 27 Nov 47   DB 9711/12
            12274-1 11 Sep 47
    (b) 2EA 12267-5 8 Dec 47

A-206 MOZART: Concerto No. 16 in D, K. 451: Excerpts (incomplete) (3ss)
        (Betty Humby, piano)
    2EA 13963-1,-1A,-2
        13964-1,-1A,-2,-3 10 Jun 49   Unpublished - not repeated
        13966-1,-1A,-2

A-207 MOZART: Concerto in C major, K. 299 (6ss)   Δ
        (René le Roy, flute; Lily Laskine, harp)

    2EA 12167-1, 68-2 11 Jul 47   HMV DB 6485/7   Vic. 12-0803/5
        12169-3 12 Jul 47   DB 9159/61   in M-1292
        12170-1, 71-2, 72-1 12 Jul 47

    Unissued take, side 3: 12169-1, 11 Jul 47

A-208 MOZART: Concerto No. 3 in G major, K. 216 (6ss)
        (Gioconda di Vito, violin)

    2EA 13808-1, 09-1 3 May 49   HMV DB 21177/8
        13810-2A, 11-1A, 12-1, 13-2   DB 9570/2
            Rec. 4 May 49

A-209 MOZART: Concerto No. 4 in D major, K. 218 (6ss)
        (Jascha Heifetz, violin)

    2EA 12521-1, 22-2, 23-2,   HMV DB 6678/80   Vic. 12-0625/7
        24-2, 25-2, 26-1   DB 9336/8   in M-1267
        Rec. 10 Nov 47   HMV FALP-136   Vic. LM-1051
                                               Sera. 60162

A-210 MOZART: Divertimento No. 2 in D, K. 131[3] (6ss)   Δ
    2EA 12585-5 4 Jan 48   HMV DB 6649/51
        12587-2, 90-1, 86-2 28/30 Nov 47   DB 9354/6
        12668-1 4 Jan 48
        12591-1 28/30 Nov 47   Vic. LHMV-1030

A-211 MOZART: Divertimento No. 15 in B-flat, K. 287: Excerpts (2ss)

    2EA 12173-1,-2 (Theme & Vars.)   Unpublished
        12174-1,-2 (Minuet)
        Rec. 12 Jul 47

A-212 MOZART: Ein Deutsches Kriegslied, K. 539 (1s)
        (Trevor Anthony, baritone)

    2EA 12165-1,-2 7 Jul 47   Unpublished

----

[1] Orchestrated by Norman del Mar.

[2] Scherzo is that movement from the Octet in Mendelssohn's orchestration which he added to the First Symphony for his first appearances in London.

[3] Omits 1st minuet, plays 5th movement before 4th and interpolates minuet from Divertimento, K. 287 on Side 5.

RPO Recordings, 1946-1952

A-213 MOZART: Symphony No. 27 in G, K. 199 (3ss)

2EA 12504-3 4 Jan 48	Vic. 12-0592B,
12505-3 8 Dec 47	12-0593
12506-2 5/6 Nov 47	in M-1264

Unissued takes, Pt.1: 12504-1 5/6 Nov 47; 12504-2,-4 (4 Jan 48)
              Pt.2: 12505-1,-2 5/6 Nov 47; 12505-3 (8 Dec 47)
              Pt.3: 12506-1 Nov. 5/6, 1947

A-214 MOZART: Magic Flute, K. 620: Overture (2ss)

2EA 14040-2, 41-2 27 Jun 49   HMV DB 21023

A- 215 MOUSSORGSKY: Khovantchina: Dance of the Persian Slaves (2ss)

2EA 11628-1 5 Feb 47   HMV DB 6450   Vic. 12-0239
    11629-4 29 Mar 47

Unissued takes, S.2: 11629-1,-2 5 Feb 47
                     11629-3 29 Mar 47

A-216 OFFENBACH: The Tales of Hoffmann[1] (30ss) (with Sadler's Wells Chorus)

Rec. 1949 from film soundtrack	Decca AX 497/511	
	Decca LXT-2582/4	Lon. LLPA-4
(with Robert Rounseville, Dorothy	Decca ACL-177/8	Lon. A-4302
Bond, Margherita Grandi, Anne Ayars,		Turn. THS-65012/14
Monica Sinclair, Owen Brannigan, Murray Dickie)		

A-217 PAISIELLO: Nina: Overture (2ss)

2EA 11666-3, 67-3 7 Jul 47   HMV DB 6499   Vic. 12-0591
                                                    in M-1264

Unissued takes, Pt.1: 11666-1 23 Feb 47
                      11666-2 7 Jul 47
                Pt.2: 11667-1 23 Feb 47
                      11667-2 7 Jul 47

A-218 ROSSINI: Pastorelli della alpi (1s)
        (Elda Ribetti, soprano; Philharmonia Orchestra)

OEA 11520-1,-2,-3   18 Dec 46   Unpublished

A-219 SAINT-SAENS: Omphale's Spinning Wheel (2ss)

2EA 11475-3, 76-4 22 Apr 47   HMV DB 6498   Vic. 12-0152

A-220 SIBELIUS: Symphony No. 2 in D, Op. 43 (10ss)

2EA 11531-2, 32-2, 33-1 21 Dec 46   HMV DB 6588/92   Vic. 12-1035/9
    11534-4 8/9 Feb 47   DB 9242/6   in M-1334
    11535-4 1 Apr 47   (Finale,exc.)in HMV ALP 1870/1 & Ang.3621B
    11536-3, 37-4 8/9 Feb 47
    11538-1, 39-2, 40-1 23/24 Dec 46

A-221 SIBELIUS: Symphony No. 6 in D, Op. 104 (6ss)   *CDM7 64027-2* △

2EA 10668-5, 69-3 10 Sep 47   HMV DB 6640/2
    10677-2 8 Jul 47   DB 9466/8
    10667-2 27 May 47
    10678-2 8 Jul 47
    10679-3 11 Nov 47

   Rec. Kingsway Hall

A-222 SIBELIUS: Tapiola, Op. 112 (4ss)

2EA 11435-2, 36-2, 37-1, 38-1   HMV DB 6412/3   Vic. 12-0948/9
    Rec. 25 Nov 46   in M-1311
                                                         Vic. LM-9001

----

[1]According to AG the film begins with an unidentified composer's ballet entitled
  "Enchanted Dragonfly" which is not by Offenbach and is not on the released discs
  but is played by the RPO. No confirmation if Beecham conducts.

RPO Recordings, 1946-1952

A-223 SMETANA: The Bartered Bride: Excerpts (4ss)
      (a) Overture (2ss)
      (b) Polka (1s)
      (c) Dance of the Comedians (1s)

(a) 2EA 11616-4	29 Mar 47	(b)(c) HMV DB 6454	Vic. 12-0813/14
11617-1	3 Feb 47	(b)(c) HMV 7r 102	in M-1294 △
(b) 2EA 11632-3	11 Apr 47		
(c) 2EA 11618-1	3 Feb 47		

A-224 STRAUSS: Ariadne auf Naxos: Final Scene (7ss)
      (Maria Cebotari, soprano; Carl Friedrich, tenor, and Field-Hyde,
        Furmedge, Garside)

2EA 12419-1,-2	13 Oct 47	Unpublished	in WSA 509/12
12420-1,-2	13 Oct 47		
12420-3,-4	15 Oct 47		
12421-1,-2	14 Oct 47		
12421-3	15 Oct 47		
12422-1,-2,-3	14 Oct 47		
12423-1,-2	14 Oct 47		
12424-1,-2	14 Oct 47		
12425-1,-2	14 Oct 47		

A-225 STRAUSS: Der Bürger als Edelmann: Op. 60: Incidental Music[1] (6ss)   △

2EA 11661-2	23 Feb 47	HMV DB 6646/8 *CDM7 63106-2*
11662-4	24 Mar 47	DB 9416/8
11663-4	5 Nov 47	
11748-2	24 Mar 47	
11749-5	5/6 Nov 47	
12507-7	20 Mar 48	

Unpublished takes: S.2 11662-1,-2   23 Feb 47
                     S.3 11663-1,-2   23 Feb 47
                     S.5 11749-1,-2   24 Mar 47
                          11749-3,-4   29 Mar 47

A-226 STRAUSS: Don Quixote, Op. 35 (10ss)   *CDM7 63106-2*   △
      (Paul Tortelier, cello; Leonard Rubens, ~~violin~~) viola)

2EA 12365-1, 66-1, 67-2, 68-1	HMV DB 6796/800
(Rec. 4 Oct 47)	DB 9357/61
12369-2 7 Oct 47	(Finale) in HMV ALP 1870/1 & Ang. 3621B
12370-1 4 Oct 47	
12371-3 8 Oct 47	
12372-1 7 Oct 47	
12373-2 8 Oct 47	
12374-4 20 Mar 48	

A-227 STRAUSS: Ariadne auf Naxos: Overture (Orig. 1912 version) (1s)

      2EA 12440-1,-2   15 Oct 47   Unpublished

A-228 STRAUSS: Elektra, Op. 58: Closing Scene (8ss)   △
      (Erna Schlüter, Ljuba Welitsch, Paul Schoeffler, Walter Widdop,
        Ernst Erbach, RPO Chorus)

2EA 12456-2, 57-2, 58-1, 59-2	HMV DB 9393/6	Vic. 12-0471/4
(Rec. 27 Oct 47)		in M-1247
12460-2 28 Oct 47		Vic. LCT-1135
12461-1, 62-2, 63-3 29 Oct 47		Rococo 1005[2]

Unpublished takes: S.5 12460-1
                     S.8 12463-1   Rec. 28 Oct 47

---

[1] Includes sections 1, 2, 3, 4, 8 and 9.

[2] Rococo incorporates this recording into their release of the entire opera from concert performances of October, 1947. Entire work may have been recorded, however programme for concert performances of 24 & 26 October indicate only the final scene was scheduled for recording at the time the programme was printed.

RPO Recordings, 1946-1952

A-229 STRAUSS: Feuersnot: Love Scene (2ss)

    2EA 11837-2, 38-2   11 Apr 47   HMV DB 21301   Vic. 12-0289
                                    (45RPM)HMV 7er 5014

A-230 STRAUSS: Ein Heldenleben, Op. 40 (10ss)   Δ

    2EA 12464-4, 12537-2 21 Nov 47   HMV DB 6620/4   Vic. 12-0988/92
       12639-1, 12637-2 14 Dec 47   DB 9204/8   in M-1321
       12465-4, 12538-2 21 Nov 47   Vic. LM-1059
       12539-2   21 Nov 47
       12575-1, 12576-2 28 Nov 47
       12638-1   14 Dec 47

A-231 (a) STRAUSS: Intermezzo, Op. 72: Interlude (1½ss)
      (b) STRAUSS: Der Bürger als Edelmann: No. 5, Minuet (½s)

    (a) 2EA 12437-2   HMV DB 6643   Vic. 12-0735
    (a)(b) 2EA 12438-1   13 Oct 47   (45RPM)HMV 7er 5014

A-232 STRAUSS: Salome, Op. 54: Dance of the Seven Veils (2ss)

    2EA 12310-3, 11-3   19 Sep 47   HMV DB 21149   Vic. 12-0344
                                       (45RPM)HMV 7r 103

A-233 (a) TCHAIKOVSKY: Romeo and Juliet, Op. 78 (5ss)
      (b) CHABRIER: Marche Joyeuse (1s)

    (a) 2EA 11470-7 8 Feb 47   HMV DB 6420/2 (b)Vic. 12-0810B
       11471-2, 72-1, 73-1, 74-1   DB 9109/11   in M-1295
          Rec. 2 Dec 46
    (b) 2EA 11384-1 6 Nov 46   (b) in HMV ALP 1870/1 & Ang. 3621B

A-234 TCHAIKOVSKY: Symphony No. 3 in D, Op. 29: 5th Movement (2ss)

    2EA 11649-1,-2   Unpublished
       11650-1,-2   9 Feb 47

A-235 TCHAIKOVSKY: Symphony No. 3 in D, Op. 29 (10ss)

    2EA 11826-2,27-2,28-2 8 Apr 47   HMV DB 6583/7   Vic. 12-0693/7
       11806-2 12 May 47   DB 9237/41   in M-1279
       11847-1,48-1,49-2 18 Apr 47
       11834-2,35-1,36-1 11 Apr 47

    Unpublished takes: Mvmt 2 Pt.2,Mvmt 3 Pt.1: 2EA 11807-1,
                                          11808-1,-2   1 Apr 47

A-236 VERDI: Macbeth: Excerpts (4ss)
      (a) Act IV: Sleepwalking Scene[1] (3ss)
      (b) Act II: La luce langue (1s)
        (Margherita Grandi, Ernest Frank, Vera Terry)

    (a) 2EA 12341-4, 12328-4, 29-4   HMV DB 6739/40
       Rec. 16 Jan 48
    (b) 2EA 12330-1 29 Sep 47

    Unpublished takes: (a) Pt.2 12328-1,-2 16 Jan 48
                    Pt.3 12329-1,-2 27 Sep 47; 12329-3 16 Jan 48
            (b) 12330-2 29 Sep 47

A-237 WAGNER: Tannhäuser: Introduction to Act 3 (2ss)

    2EA 11645-1,-2 8 Feb 47   Unpublished
       11633-1,-2 5 Feb 47

----

[1]The Final high "D" is sung by Dorothy Bond.

RPO Recordings, 1946-1952

A-238 WAGNER: Das Rheingold: Entrance of the Gods into Valhalla (2ss)
        (Paul Schoeffler, P. Jones, G. Chitty, N. Evans, M. Field-Hyde,
        G. Garside, E. Furmedge)

   2EA 12315-1,-2,-3
       12316-1,-2,-3   22 Sep 47   Unpublished

A-239 WAGNER: Das Rheingold: Entrance of the Gods into Valhalla (2ss)
        (W. Widdop, M. Field-Hyde, G. Garside, E. Furmedge, T. Hermann,
        G. Chitty, S. Patris)

   2EA 12472-1,-2
       12473-1,-2   28 Oct 47   Unpublished

                          END OF RPO LISTING

Since the above was completed, new information about alternate takes has been
received, too late for inclusion in the body of the discography. This information
is included below; where no date is indicated, it is the same date as the issued
take shown in the body of the discography. All prefixes 2EA. Semicolon separates date.

A-134 9024-2; 9025-2; 9026-2 (15/17 Aug); 9026-3 (15/17 Aug); 9026-4,-5; 9028-2,-3;
       9030-2,-3; 9031-2
A-135 9042-1,-2 (24 Aug); 9043-2
A-137 9030-2,-3; 9040-2,-3, 9041-2,-3; 9044-2
A-143 9045-2; 10653-1,-2 (17 Oct); 10653-6; 10654-2, 10655-2, 10656-1 (17 Oct);
       10659-1,-2 (24 Oct)
A-145 9032-1 (17 Aug); 9032-2,-3 (23 Oct); 9032-5, 9033-2, 9034-2, 9035-2, 9036-2,
       9038-2
A-146 10658-2, 10661-2
A-150 10381-1, 10382-1, 10383-1, 10384-1
A-152 10789-1,-2 (5 Dec); 10789-3B,3C (new master 16 Apr 47); 10789-4
A-155 10788-2; 10662-2
A-160 11842-1,-2 (14 Apr); 11843-1,-2 (14 Apr); 11843-3
A-162 12635-2,-3; 12636-1,-2 (alternate matrix Pt. 2, rec. 14 Dec); 12640-1; 12641-1,-3
A-163 12331-1; 12332-2; 12333-1,-2; 12334-2; 12335-1, 12336-1 12337-2,-3; 12338-2
A-164 11382-2,-3,-3A; 11383-1A,-2
A-165 10680-1,-2,-3 (10 Sep); 10680-4; 10681-1, 10682-1, 10683-2
A-166 11439-1,-2 (25 Nov 46); 11439-3; 11440-1,-2 (25 Nov 46); 11440-3,-4; 11441-1;
       11442-2
A-167 Also -2 for all sides
A-168 11530-2,-3
A-170 11318-4; 11320-3 (4 Dec); 11320-4, 11321-3, 11322-4
A-178 11328-1,-2 (30 Oct 46); 11328-4
A-182 13614-1, 13615-1, 13613-2
A-183 Also -1 for all sides
A-185 Not checked for alternate takes
A-187 11646-1,-2,-4; 11647-1,-2 (8/9 Feb); 11647-3, 12275-1,-2; 12276-1, 12277-1 (15
       Sep); 12278-2
A-189 Not checked for alternate takes
A-194 Not checked for alternate takes
A-195 12262-2 also
A-199 12312-1,-2 (22 Sep); 12313-2, 12314-2; 11648-1,-2 (9 Feb)
A-200 11630-2
A-203 11454-1 (28 Nov); 11454-2,-4; 11619-4
A-205 12268-2; 12269-1,-2 (11 Sep); 12269-3, 12274-2, 12267-1,-2,-3 (11 Sep); 12267-4
A-207 12167-2, 12167-3 (12 Jul); 12168-1, 12169-2, 12170-2, 12171-1, 12172-2; 12167-3
       (12 Jul)
A-210 12585-4, 12668-2
A-215 11628-2
A-219 11475-1,-2,-4; 11476-1,-2 (2 Dec 46); 11476-3,-5 (18 Apr 47)
A-220 11531-1,-3; 11532-1; 11534-1,-2 (23/24 Dec 46); 11534-3; 11535-1,-2 (23/24 Dec 46);
       11535-3 (1 Apr 47); 11536-1 (23/24 Dec 46); 11536-2, 11537-1,-2 (23/24 Dec 46);
       11537-3, 11538-2, 11539-1, 11540-2
A-221 10668-1,-2 (27 May 47); 10668-3,-4; 10669-1 (27 May 47); 10669-2,-4; 10677-1;
       10667-1 (27 May 47); 10678-1; 10679-1,-2 (8 Jul 47)
A-222 11435-1, 11436-1, 11437-2, 11438-2

RPO Recordings, 1946-1952

A-223 11616-1,-2 (3 Feb 47); 11616-3, 11617-2; 11632-1,-2 (5 Feb 47); 11632-4;
     11616-4; 11618-2
A-225 11661-1; 11662-3 (24 Mar); 11663-3; 11748-1; 11749-6,-7,-8; 12507-1,-2,-3
     (5 Nov 47); 12507-4,-5,-6
A-226 12365-2; 12366-2; 12367-1; 12368-2; 12368-3,-4 (20 Mar 48); 12369-1,-3;
     12370-2; 12371-1,-2 (4 Oct); 12372-2; 12373-1; 12374-1,-2 (8 Oct 47);
     12374-3,-5; 12367-3 (8 Oct 47)
A-228 12456-1; 12457-1; 12458-2; 12459-1; 12462-1; 12463-2 (28 Oct)
A-229 11837-1; 11838-1
A-230 12464-1,-2 (29 Oct); 12464-3; 12537-1, 12639-2,-3; 12637-1; 12465-1 (29 Oct);
     12465-2,-3; 12538-1; 12539-1; 12638-2
A-231 12437-1; 12438-2
A-232 12310-1,-2; 12311-1,-2
A-233 11470-1,-2 (2 Dec 46); 11470-3 (16 Dec); 11470-4,-5 (19 Dec); 11470-6; 11471-1;
     11472-2; 11473-2; 11474-2; 11384-2,-2A
A-235 11826-1; 11827-1; 11828-1; 11806-1 (1 Apr 47); 11834-1; 11835-2
A-236 12341-1,-2 (29 Sep 47); 12341-3

The following letter has come to hand which sheds some light on Sir Thomas' recording activity with the L.P.O. after the war, and we will quote it in its entirety for whatever information it may contain of relevance:

THE GRAMOPHONE COMPANY, LTD.

CopY

HAYES, MIDDLESEX, ENGLAND

AIR MAIL

27th December 1945.

H.C. Darnell, Esq.,
Mgr. Royalty Dept.,
Radio Corporation of America
RCA Victor Division
Camden, New Jersey

Dear Mr. Darnell,

SIR THOMAS BEECHAM RECORDINGS

    Since Sir Thomas' arrival in this country we have held between August and the present day several recording sessions on your behalf with Sir Thomas conducting the London Philharmonic Orchestra. We are therefore giving you below a complete statement of the repertoire recorded, showing what Sir Thomas has thus far approved as suitable for issue.

(1) Date of sessions held from August 1945.

Date	No. of Sessions
August 15th	2
" 17th	1
" 20th	2
" 24th	2
October 3rd	1/3
" 17th	2
" 23rd	2
" 24th	1
December 5th	2
" 27th	2

Several other dates were booked but were cancelled by Sir Thomas Beecham.

(2) Recordings approved from commencement of contract

        Schubert - 6th Symphony
        Haydn - No. 97 Symphony
        Handel-Beecham Concerto (1 side to be approved)
        Beethoven - 4th Symphony
        Prince Igor Overture
        Die Entfuhrung - Serail
        Les Troyens - Royal Hunt & Storm
        Les Troyens - Trojan March.

RPO Recordings, 1946-1952

(3) <u>Recorded but rejected - to be repeated 27.12.45</u>

> Handel-Beecham Concerto w/Lady Beecham (1 side)
> Great Elopement Ballet (1 side only)

(4) <u>Recorded but rejected and not to be repeated</u>

> Rhinegold - Entry of the Gods
> Salome - Salome's Dance (only one side recorded)

No doubt Sir Thomas will explain to you the difficulties which arose in connection with the "Rhinegold" and "Salome" excerpts. All through we have maintained that Sir Thomas shall be the sole arbiter as to whether the artistic standard of the orchestra was such that he considered he could obtain recordings which he would finally approve.

(5) <u>Repertoire to be recorded 27.12.45</u>

> Mozart Overtures - Schauspieldirektor (same as Impressario)
>   Cosi fan Tutte
>   Tito
>   Idomeneo (possibly)
>
> Repeats - Handel-Beecham Concerto (1 side)
>   Great Elopement (1 side)

We are arranging to record on acetate and wax and hope to secure Sir Thomas' approval of the acetate recordings after completion of the session.

(6) <u>-Repertoire in Appendix to Agreement</u>

> From the above information you will see that the only works given in the agreement which have not been recorded are:

> Idomeneo (if not made on 27.12.45)
> Ravel - Alborado del Grazioso
> J. Strauss - Good Old Times Waltz

With regard to the "Good Old Times Waltz" Sir Thomas says he cannot trace this waltz and has recorded in its place the Waltz and Polonaise from "Eugen Onegin."

(7) <u>Additional repertoire agreed (not yet recorded)</u>

> Mozart - Requiem
> Dvorak - Golden Spinning Wheel

(8) <u>Additional repertoire recorded and approved</u>

> Eine Kleine Nachtmusik

(9) <u>Payments made to Orchestra</u>

> We have completed the payment called for under the agreement i.e. 8 sessions @ ₤270 each and 3 sessions @ ₤210 each. All subsequent sessions have been free and no other payments made to the orchestra.

> The arrangements with Sir Thomas have been on the most cordial lines and he is returning to the U.S.A. tomorrow the 28th instant, which is some weeks earlier than he anticipated.

> You will no doubt appreciate that the large number of sessions has been due to Sir Thomas' insistence on securing a perfect artistic result and we trust that you will be pleased with the results secured.

(10) <u>L.P.O. Agreement</u>

> We were unable to secure an extension of the expiry date of this agreement so that effectively the contract with the orchestra expired on the 1st November 1945.

> The Invoice for all expenditure will be sent to you in the course of a few days.

> Finally, shells of all approved recordings will be rushed to you as quickly as possible.

> Yours very truly,

> C.H. Thomas

<u>SECTION V</u>

THE RECORDINGS FOR COLUMBIA PHONOGRAPH CO.(USA) AND PHILIPS (ENGLAND), 1949-1958

Part 1: <u>The Columbia Symphony Orch. Recordings, 1949</u>

A-240 BIZET: Carmen: Orchestral Suite (Arr. Beecham) (4ss)   Δ

      xco 42162, 65, 63, 64[1]   Col. 72962/3-D[4]

      Rec. 21 Dec 49

	in MX-333
Col. CX-1037	Col. ML-4287
Phi. GL-5720	Odys. 32-16-0117
Font. KFR-4001	(exc) in Col.AAL-27
Font. CFL-1042	(45RPM) Col. A-333

A-241 NICOLAI: The Merry Wives of Windsor: Overture (2ss)

      xco 42170/1   Col. 73051-D

      Rec. 27 Dec 49

Phi. GL-5693	Col. ML-2134
Font. CFL-1033	Col. AAL-5
	Col. CB-1

A-242 PONCHIELLI: La Gioconda: Dance of the Hours (2ss)

      xco 42172/3

      Rec. 27 Dec 49

Col. LX-1554	Col. 73052-D
Phi. GL-5692	Col. ML-2134
Phi. GL-5693	Col. AAL-5
Font. CFL-1021	Odys. 32-16-0117
	Col. ML-5171

A-243 TCHAIKOVSKY: Capriccio Italien, Op. 45 (4ss)

      xco 42166, 69, 67, 68   Col. LX-8924/5   Col. 72964/5-D

      Rec. 22 Dec 49   in MX-334

Col. CX-1037	Col. ML-4287
Phi. GL-5720	Odys. 32-16-0117
Font. KFR-4001	

Part 2: <u>The RPO & Philadelphia Orchestra Recordings, 1950-1958</u>

A-244 ARNELL: Punch and the Child, Op. 49 (5ss)   Δ

      [3]CAX 10841-1A, 42-1A, 43-1B,   Col. LX-1391/3S *Kingsway Hall*

          44-1A, 45-1A   CBS 61431   Col. ML-4593

      Rec. 31 May, 1 Jun 50

A-245 (a) BALAKIREV: Thamar: Symphonic Poem   *CDM7 63375-2*   Δ

      (b) DVORAK: Symphonic Variations, Op. 78   Δ

      (a) Rec. 6 Apr 1954 *Walthamstow*. Phi. ABL-3047   Col. ML-4974

      (b) Rec. Dec. 1953   Phi. GL-5717

A-246 BEETHOVEN: Coriolan Overture, Op. 62

      Rec. December 1953 *Walthamstow* Phi. A-03626   Col. ML-5029

                               Phi. SBR-6218

                                Phi. SBR-6244

                                Phi. ABL-3247

                                Phi. GL-5714

----

[1]This was the "friendship" record with which Beecham ended his feud with Columbia which had begun with the lawsuit over the N.Y. Philharmonic Recordings in 1942.

[2]Mislabeled as R.P.O. on ML-5171.

[3]Most of the matrix numbers for 78RPM editions in this section have little significance, due to the recordings having been mainly of tape origin.

[4]Excerpts also on 78 RPM Columbia J-211, matrix Co 51135-36.

Columbia Recordings, 1950-1958

A-247 BEETHOVEN: Symphony No. 3 in E-flat, Op. 55

      Rec. 20 Dec 51   Col. CX-1086   Col. ML-4698
        Abbey Road.   ·Phi. SBL-5233 (excerpts) Col. XLP-14889[2]

A-248 BEETHOVEN: Symphony No. 6 in F, Op. 68

      Rec. 7,15,18,19 Dec 51,   Col. CX-1062   Col. ML-4828
       5 May 52   Phi. GL-5730
                       Font. KFR-4003

A-249 BEETHOVEN: Symphony No. 8 in F, Op. 93

                                   CDM7 63398-1 Δ

      Rec. 18 May 51,   Col. CX-1039   Col. ML-4681
       8 Oct 51,   Phi. GL-5745   Col. CB-21
       16 & 27 Nov 51   Font. CFL-1004
      Kingsway Hall.   Font. EFL-2507

A-250 BERLIOZ: Harold in Italy, Op. 16   *MPK 47679*   Δ
       (William Primrose, vla.)

      Rec. 13 & 15 Nov 51   Col. CX-1019   Col. ML-4542
      Kingsway Hall.   Phi. GL-5715   Odys. Y-33286
                     Font. KFR-4002 (exc.) Col. XLP 9883-2[4]

A-251 BERLIOZ: Overtures   Δ
       (a) Waverly, Op. 2   Rec. 2 & 3 Dec 54
       (b) King Lear, Op. 4   Rec. 2 & 3 Dec 54   *MPK 47679*
       (c) Les Francs-Juges Rec. 17 Dec 54
       (d) Le Corsaire, Op. 21 Rec. 2 & 3 Dec 54
       (e) Roman Carnival, Op. 9 Rec. 16 Dec 54   *MPK 47679*

         Walthamstow.   Phi. ABL-3083   Col. ML-5064
                      Phi. GL-5633   Odys. Y-33287
         (b)(c)Phi. SBR-6243   (d) in Col. XSM 158111[5]
          (e)Phi. SBR-6244; GL-5714

A-252 BERLIOZ: Te Deum, Op. 22[1]   Δ
       (A. Young, ten.; LPO Choir, Dulwich Boys Choir, Denis Vaughan, organ)

      Rec. Dec. 1953   Phi. ABL-3006   Col. ML-4897
      Hornsey Parish Church. Phi. GL-5637   Odys. 32-16-0206

A-253 BERLIOZ: Les Troyens: Excerpts   Δ
       (a) Overture
       (b) March

       (a) Rec. 16 Dec 54   Phi. GL-5714   Col. ML-5321
       (b) Rec. Dec. 1953   Phi. SBR-6215   Odys. Y-33288
         & 3 Nov 58   *Walthamstow.* (b) in Col. XSM 158111[5]

A-254 BERNERS: The Triumph of Neptune: Ballet Suite   Δ
       (R. Grooters, bar.; Philadelphia Orchestra)

      Rec. 3 Feb 52   CBS 61431   Col. ML-4593
                             (exc.) Col. XLP 11372[3]

A-255 BIZET: Fair Maid of Perth: Suite, Arr. Beecham (4ss)   Δ

      CAX 10708-1, 09-1,   Col. LX-8790/1
           10-1, 11-1   Phi. GL-5693   Col. ML-2133
      Rec. 6 Feb 50   Font. EFR-2029
       Abbey Road   Font. CFL-1033

----

[1] Omits ad lib movements 3 and 8.

[2] Columbia Masterwork Preview #20; includes comments on recording by David
  Randolph, and excerpts from 1st, 3rd and 4th movements.

[3] Columbia Masterwork Preview #12: excerpt.

[4] Columbia Masterwork Preview #9: excerpt.

[5] Columbia Masterwork 1975 Sampler #3 (AS-111).

Columbia Recordings, 1950-1958

A-256 BOCCHERINI: Overture in D

       Rec. Dec. 1953   Phi. GL-5714   Col. ML-5029
          Walthamstow   Phi. ABL-3247
                                   Phi. SBR-6244

A-257 BRAHMS: Concerto in D major, Op. 77
         (Isaac Stern, violin)

       Rec. 5,6,7 Nov 51   Phi. GBL-5638   Col. ML-4530
          Abbey Road.   Phi. ABL-3023   (exc.) Col. XLP 9427[3]

A-258 BRAHMS: Tragic Overture, Op. 81

       Rec. Dec. 1953   Phi. GL-5714   Col. ML-5029
          Walthamstow.   Phi. ABL-3247

A-259 CHABRIER: Espana Rhapsody (2ss)   △

       CAX 10803-1B, 04-1B   Col. LX-1592
                          Phi. GL-5692   Col. ML-5171
       Rec. 24 Apr 50   Font. CFL-1021   Col. AAL-11
          Abbey Road.   Font. EFR-2029

A-260 DELIUS: Appalachia   △
         (RPO Chorus)

       Rec. 2 Dec 52   Col. CX-1112   Col. ML-4915
          Abbey Road.   Phi. GL-5690   Odys. Y-33283
                          Font. CFL-1009
                          CBS 61354

A-261 DELIUS: Arabesque   MPK 47680   △
         (Einar Nørby, bar.; BBC Chorus)

       Rec. Oct. or Nov. 1955   Phi. GL-5690   Col. ML-5268
          Walthamstow.   Font. CFL-1009
                          CBS[1]

A-262 DELIUS: Eventyr (4ss)   △

       CAX 11003-2, 11063-2,   Col. LX-8931/2
          11064-2, 11062-2   Font. CFL-1042   Col. ML-4637
       Rec. 12 Jan, 3 Apr 51   CBS 61271   Odys. Y-33284
          Abbey Road.

A-263 DELIUS: Hassan: Incidental Music   MPK 47686   △
         (L. Fry, A. Leven, Frederick Riddle, vla; BBC Chorus)
                 Leavins
       Rec. Feb. 1955(?) Oct. 23, 29 Phi. GL-5691   Col. ML-5268
          Walthamstow.   Font. CFL-1020
                          CBS 61224

            (Intermezzo & Serenade) CBS 30056

A-264 DELIUS: Koanga: Closing Scene (2ss)
         (RPO Chorus)

       CAX 11022-3, 23-2B   Col. LX-1502
       Rec. 26 Jan 51   Col. CX-1112   Col. ML-4915
          Abbey Road.   Phi. GL-5693   Odys. Y-33284
                          Font. CFL-1033
                          CBS 61271

A-265 DELIUS: Sea Drift
         (Gordon Clinton, baritone)

       Rec. 22 Jan 51 Abbey Road. Unpublished[2]

----

[1] Announced for possible reissue, summer 1975.

[2] Existing test take XAX-351-2N

[3] Columbia Masterworks Preview #8; excerpt from 1st movement.

Columbia Recordings, 1950-1958

A-266 DELIUS: In a Summer Garden

   Rec. 27 Oct 51   Col. C-1017
     Abbey Road.   Phi. GL-5713
               Phi. SBR-6242
               CBS 30056

                              △

A-267 DELIUS: A Mass of Life
   (R. Raisbeck, M. Sinclair, C. Craig, B. Boyce, LPO Choir)

   Rec. 2 Dec 52   Col. CX-1078/9   Col. SL-197
     Abbey Road.   Font. CFL-1005/6
               CBS 61182/3

                              △

A-268 DELIUS: North Country Sketches (6ss)

   CAX 11067-2, 68-2, 69-2,   Col. LX-1399/401
      70-2, 71-2, 72-2   Phi. GL-5691   Col. ML-4637
    Rec. 14 Feb ~~51~~ 49   Font. CFL-1020   Odys. Y-33283
      Abbey Road.   CBS 61354

                              △

A-269 DELIUS: Over the Hills and Far Away

   Rec. 7 Feb 50   Col. C-1017   Col. ML-5268
               Phi. GL-5713   Col. ML-2133
               Phi. SBR-6242
               CBS[1]

                              △

A-270 (a) DELIUS: Paris (Song of a Great City)
   (b) DELIUS: Sea Drift   **MPK 47680** △
     ~~(John Brownlee, bar.; LPO Choir)~~ *(Bruce Boyce, BBC Chorus, Leslie Woodgate)*

   (a) Rec. Fall 1955   Phi. ABL-3088   Col. ML-5079
   (b) Rec. 23 Apr 54 ,   (a) CBS 61271   (a) Odys. Y-33284
      2,3 Dec 54   (b) CBS 61224
      Walthamstow

                              △

A-271 (a) ELGAR: Enigma Variations, Op. 36   △
   (b) ELGAR: Cockaigne Overture, Op. 40   △
   (c) ELGAR: Serenade in E major, Op. 20   △

   (a)(b) Rec. 26,27 Nov,   Phi. GBL-5646   Col. ML-5031
      13,14 Dec 54   Phi. ABL-3053
    (c) Rec. 26,27 Nov 54   (a)Phi. SBR-6224
     Walthamstow   (b)(c)Phi. SBR-6225
           (b)CBS 30055 **CBS 61660**

A-272 FRANCK: Le Chasseur Maudit (4ss)   △

   CAX 11386-3, 87-3,   Col. LX-8813/14
      88-2, 90-4   Col. CX-1087   Col. ML-4454
    Rec. 9 May 51   Font. CFL-1042
      Kingsway Hall.   Font. KFR-4000

A-273 GOLDMARK: Rustic Wedding Symphony, Op. 26[2]

   Rec. 5,6,7,8 May 52   Col. CX-1067   Col. ML-4626
      Abbey Road.   Phi. GL-5719   (exc.) Col. XLP 12722[3]
               Phi. NBL-5041

                              △

A-274 GRETRY: Zemire et Azor: Air de Ballet

   Rec. 28 Apr 54   Phi. GL-5713   Col. ML-5029
      Walthamstow   Phi. SBR-6215
               Phi. SBR-6245

----

[1]Announced for reissue, summer 1975.

[2]Omits variations 5 and 8 of 1st movement.

[3]Columbia Masterwork Preview #14; excerpt.

Columbia Recordings, 1950-1958

A-275 HANDEL: The Faithful Shepherd: Suite, Arr. Beecham (6ss)

      CAX 10811-1A, 10915-1A, (Nos.3-6) Col. LX-1600   Col. M-990
          10916-1A; 10917-1A, Col. CX-1105   Col. ML-4374
          10918-1A, 10812-1A   Font. CFL-1008   Odys. Y-33285
          Rec. 25 Apr, 28 Sep 50   (Musette) in Col. XSM 158111[2]

A-276 HAYDN: Symphony No. 93 in D (6ss)

      CAX 10805-1D, 06-1C, Col. LX-1361/3
          07-1C, 08-1C,   Col. CX-1038   Col. ML-4374
          09-1C, 10-1C   Phi. NBL-5037   Odys. Y-33285
          Rec. 24,25 Apr 50   Phi. GL-5632

A-277 HAYDN: Symphony No. 94 in G (6ss)

      CAX 11255-4A, 56-2A, Col. LX-1499/501
          57-5A, 58-3A,   Col. CX-1104   Col. ML-4453
          59-6A, 60-4A   Phi. NBL-5037
          Rec. 13,14 Jul,   Phi. GL-5632
             8 Oct 51   *Abbey Road*

A-278 HAYDN: Symphony No. 103 in E-flat

      Rec. 29 Jan, 1 Feb 51 Col. CX-1104   Col. ML-4453
        Abbey Road.   Phi. SBR-6253

A-279 MASSENET: La Vièrge: Last Sleep of the Virgin   Δ

      Rec. 3 Nov 58 ?   Phi. GL-5713   Col. ML-5321
                   SBRG215 o   Col. PE-7 (7" 33 1/3)
                                   Odys. Y-33288

A-280 (a) MÉHUL: Timoléon: Overture
      (b) MÉHUL: Le Trésor Supposé: Overture
      (c) MÉHUL: Le Chasse de jeune Henri: Overture

      (a) Rec. 10 Feb 58   Phi. GL-5714   Col. ML-5029
        Walthamstow   (b)(c) Phi. ABR-4056
                   (b)(c) Phi. SBR-6244
                   (b)(c) Phi. SBR-6253

A-281 MENDELSSOHN: Fingal's Cave: Overture   Δ

      Rec. 7 Feb, 1 Jun 50   Phi. GL-5692 ✓   Col. AAL-7
        Abbey Road.   Font. CFL-1021   Col. CB-1
                       Font. EFR-2029

A-282 MENDELSSOHN: Ruy Blas: Overture (2ss)   Δ

      CAX 11055-1B, 56-1B   Col. LX-1584
        Rec. 16 Mar 51   Phi. GL-5692 ✓   Col. AAL-7
        Abbey Road   Font. CFL-1021   Col. CB-1

A-283 MENDELSSOHN: Symphony No. 4 in A, Op. 90 "Italian"   *CDM7-63398-1* Δ

      Rec. 8 May 52   Col. C-1006   Col. ML-4681
       Abbey Road   Phi. GL-5745
                    Font. CFL-1008
                    Font. EFL-2507

A-284 MOZART: German Dance, K. 605 (1s)   Δ

      CAX 11100-3B   Col. LX-1587
       Rec. 9 May 51   Col. SCB-106 (45RPM)
       Abbey Road.   Phi. GL-5692
                  Font. CFL-1021

---

[1]10916 carries 1B take on LX-1600.

[2]Columbia Masterwork 1975 Sampler #3 (AS-111).

Columbia Recordings, 1950-1958

A-285 MOZART: Requiem Mass in D minor, K. 626   *Walthamstow*
      (E. Morison, M. Sinclair, A. Young, M. Nowakowski, BBC Choir)

    Rec. 13-14 Dec. 1954   Font. CFL-1000   Col. ML-5160

A-286 MOZART: Symphony No. 31 in D, K. 297

    Rec. 9 Mar 51   Col. CX-1038   Col. ML-4474
      Abbey Road   Phi. SBL-5226
                      Phi. GL-5742
                      Font. EFL-2503

A-287 (a) MOZART: Symphony No. 35 in D, K. 385   *Walthamstow*
     (b) MOZART: Symphony No. 36 in C, K. 425

    (a) Rec. Dec. 1953 & May 1,   Phi. ABL-3067   Col. ML-5001
        1954   (a)Phi. GL-5742   Odys. 32-36-0009
    (b) Rec. 30 Apr, 1 May 54 (a)Font. EFL-2503

A-288 MOZART: Symphony No. 38 in D, K. 504 (6ss)

    CAX 10787-1D, 88-1B,   Col. LX-1517/9   Col. 73055/7-D
        89-1B, 90-1B,   _____   in M-934
        91-1B, 92-1C   Col. CX-1105   Col. ML-4313
    Rec. 18 Apr 50   Phi. BL-5226   Odys. 32-16-0023
      Abbey Road.   Phi. GL-5742   Odys. 32-36-0009
                      Font. EFL-2503

A-289 (a) MOZART: Symphony No. 39 in E-flat, K. 543   *Walthamstow*
     (b) MOZART: Symphony No. 40 in G minor, K. 550

    (a) Rec. Fall 1955   Phi. ABL-3094   Col. ML-5194
    (b) Rec. 27 Apr, 31 Aug 54 (a)Phi. BL-5226   Odys. 32-36-0009
                      (a)Phi. GL-5742
                      (a)Font. EFL-2503
                      (b)Font. EFL-2518

A-290 (a) MOZART: Symphony No. 41 in G minor, K. 551 (7ss)   *Abbey Road*
     (b) MOZART: March in D, K. 249 (1s)

    (a) CAX 10724-1A, 25-1A,   Col. LX-1337/40   (b) Col. 73048-D
        26-1A, 27-1A,   (b)Col. LX-1587   in M-933
        28-1B, 29-1B,   (a)Col. C-1002   (a) Col. ML-4313
        30-1A   (a)Font. EFL-2518   (a) Odys. 32-16-0023
    Rec. 22 Feb 50   (b)Font. CFL-1042   (a) Odys. 32-36-0009
    (b) CAX 10731-1B   (b)Col. SCB-106(45RPM)
      Rec. ca. 22 Feb 50

A-291 RIMSKY-KORSAKOV: Le Coq d'Or Suite   *Kingsway Hall.*

    Rec. 9, 15 Jan 51   Col. CX-1087   Col. ML-4454
    (March on ML-5321 and   Phi. GL-5692 ✓   (March) Col. ML-5321
    Odys. Y-33288 rec.   Font. KFR-4000   "   Odys. Y-33288
    2 Apr 56)   Font. CFL-1021

A- 292 ROSSINI: La Cambiale di Matrimonio: Overture (2ss) *ℓ Abbey Road.* ... Δ
    CAX 10919-1C, 20-2C   Col. LX-1458   *700 RESONANT !*
    Rec. 28 Sep 50   Phi. GL-5693   Col. AAL-11
                      Font. CFL-1033   Col. CB-1

A-293 ROSSINI: Semiramide: Overture
      (Philadelphia Orchestra)
    Rec. 3 Feb 52   Phi. GL-5693   Col. AAL-27
                      Font. CFL-1033   Col. CB-1

44

Columbia Recordings, 1950-1958

A-294 (a) SCHUBERT: Symphony No. 1 in D, D.82
       (b) SCHUBERT: Symphony No. 2 in B-flat, D.125

      (a) Rec. Dec. 1953   Phi. ABL-3001   Col. ML-4903
      (b) Rec. 28 Apr 54   Phi. GL-5634
         Walthamstow

A-295 SCHUBERT: Symphony No. 8 in B minor, D.759 (6ss)   *CDM7 63398-2*   △

     CAX 10996-2C, 97-1C,   Col. LX-8942/4
          98-2B,[   ]1   Col. CX-1039   Col. ML-4474
       11018-4D, 19-5F   Phi. GL-5730   Col. CB-21
                  Font. EFL-2505 (exc.) Col. XLP 11369[4]
      Rec. 15 Jan,   Font. CFL-1004
         11,23 Jul 51   Font. EFR-2002
      Abbey Road.

A-296 SCHUMANN: Manfred, Op. 115
      (J. Balcon, R. de la Torre, L. Browne, D. Enders: actors;[2]
      G. Holt, C. Duchesneau, N. Miller: singers; BBC Chorus)

      Rec. 13,14,17,20,   Font. CFL-1026/7   Col. M2L-245
        22,23 Dec 54 (Over.)in Font. CFL-1042
      Walthamstow

A-297 SIBELIUS: Concerto in D, Op. 47 (7ss)
      (Isaac Stern, violin)

     CAX 11481-5A, 82-4A, 83-4A, Col. LX-8747/50S
          84-2A, 85-3A, 86-3A, Col. C-1008   Col. ML-4550
          87-4A   Phi. GL-5718   (exc.) Col. XLP 12419[5]
       Rec. 5,6,7, Nov 51   Phi. NBL-5030
       Abbey Road.

A-298 SIBELIUS: Four Historical Scenes, Op. 25   *CDM7 63397-2*   △

      Rec. 28 Sep 50 &   Col. C-1018   Col. ML-4550
        8 May 52   Phi. GL-5718   (exc.) Col. XLP 12419[5]
       Abbey Road.   Phi. NBL-5030

A-299 SIBELIUS: Karelia, Op. 11: March   △

      Rec. Dec. 1953   Phi. GL-5716   Col. ML-5321
       Walthamstow   Phi. SBR-6215   Odys. Y-33288

A-300 SIBELIUS: Symphony No. 1 in E minor, Op. 39

      Rec. 23 May 51,   Col. CX-1085   Col. ML-4653
        17, 27 Nov 51,   Phi. GL-5716
        5,7 Dec 51,   Phi. SBR-6245
        5 May 52
       Abbey Road

A-301 SIBELIUS: The Tempest, Op. 109: Suite[3]   *CDM7 63397-2* △

      Rec. Fall 1955   Phi. ABR-4045 (exc.) in Col. ML-5321
       Abbey Road.   Canon   "   Odys. Y-33288
             Scene SBR6215 o

A-302 STRAUSS, J.: Morning Papers Waltz, Op. 249 (2ss)   △

     CAX 10712-1B, 716-1A   Col. LX-1322   Col. 73053-D
       Rec. 6,7 Feb 50   Phi. GL-5692   Col. ML-2134
       Abbey Road   Font. CFL-1021   Col. AAL-6

---

[1] Matrix number missing from "Voices of the Past" index.

[2] DV states that labelling credits G. Rylands, whose voice does not appear on the issued discs.

[3] Movements recorded: The Oak-Tree, Humoresque, Caliban's Song, Canon, Scene, Berceuse, The Storm (Prelude), Chorus of the Winds, Intermezzo, Dance of the Nymphs, Prospero, Song of Miranda, Naiads and Dance. The ownership of this recording is currently in doubt, which may account for its failure to be reissued in toto, although several unnamed excerpts appeared in Col. ML-5321 and on Odyssey Y-33288.

[4] Columbia Records Preview; excerpts from 1st movement

[5] Columbia Masterwork Preview; excerpts.

Columbia Recordings, 1950-1958

A-303 SUPPÉ: Morning, Noon and Night in Vienna (2ss)   1\

    CAX 10793-5A, 94-2A   Col. LX-1438   Col. 73054-D
                                 Phi. GL-5692   Col. ML-2134
    Rec. 24 Apr 50   Font. CFL-1021   Col. ML-5171
    Abbey Road.   Col. AAL-6
                                                       Col. CB-1

A-304 TCHAIKOVSKY: Nutcracker Suite, Op. 71a   CDM7 63380-2   Δ

    Rec. Dec. 1953   Phi. SBR-6213   Col. ML-5171
    Walthamstow   Phi. ABL-3247 (Waltz) Col. ML-4872

                        (Russian Dance, Chinese Dance, Sugar Plum Fairy)
                                     in   Col. PE-17(7" 33 1/3)

A-305 TCHAIKOVSKY: Symphony No. 2 in C, Op. 17   Δ

    Rec. Dec. 1953   Phi. ABL-3015   Col. ML-4872
    Walthamstow   Phi. GL-5636

A-306 WAGNER: Orchestral Excerpts   Walthamstow
        (a) Parsifal: Good Friday Spell
        (b) Flying Dutchman: Overture
        (c) Götterdämmerung: Rhine Journey & Funeral Music
        (d) Die Meistersinger: Prelude to Act 3; Dance of the Apprentices and
            Entrance of the Mastersingers

    (a) Rec. Dec. 1953   Phi. ABL-3039   Col. ML-4962
    (b) Rec. 16 Apr 54   Phi. GL-5635
    (c) Rec. Dec. 1953, 20 Apr 54
    (d) Rec. 17 Apr 54
A-307 WAGNER: Lohengrin: Prelude to Act 1 (2ss)   Abbey Road.

    CAX 11572-2, 73-2   Col. LX-1557
    Rec. 20 Dec 51

                        END OF COLUMBIA LISTING

SECTION VI

THE RECORDINGS FOR EMI (ENGLAND) & RCA (USA), 1955-1959[1]

(with Royal Philharmonic Orchestra unless otherwise noted)

A-308 BALAKIREV: Symphony No. 1 in C   *CDM7 63375-2*   ⚠

    Rec. Nov. & Dec. 1956   Col. CX-1450   Ang. 35399; S-35399
    Abbey Road.   HMV XLP 30002; SXLP 30002   Sera. 60062; S-60062[2]
                               HMV SXLP-30171*

A-309 BEETHOVEN: Mass in C, Op. 86
      (Jennifer Vyvyan, sop.; Monica Sinclair, con.; Richard Lewis, ten,
      Marian Nowakowski, bs.; Beecham Choral Society, Denis Vaughan, dir.)

    Rec. May & Nov. 1956,   HMV ALP-1674; ASD-280   Cap. G-7168; SG-7168
      April 1958   *Abbey Road.*

A-310 (a) BEETHOVEN: Symphony No. 2 in D, Op. 36   *CDM7 69811-2*   ⚠
    (b) BEETHOVEN: The Ruins of Athens: Overture & Incidental Music *CDM7 64871-2* ⚠

    (a) Rec. Mar. 1957, *Abbey Road.* HMV ALP-1596; ASD-287   Ang. 35509; S-35509
        Mar. & Sep. 1956   HMV HQS-1154*
    (b) Rec. Mar. & Oct. 1957   (b,Ov.)HMV SXLP-30158*

A-311 BEETHOVEN: Symphony No. 7 in A, Op. 92   *CDM7 69871-2*   ⚠

    Mono rec. Oct.1957 &   HMV ALP-1748; ASD -311   Cap. G-7223; SG-7223
      Oct 1958 *Salle Wagram.*
    Stereo rec. July 1959   *Abbey Road.*

A-312 BERLIOZ: The Damnation of Faust: Minuet of the Will-o-the wisps *CDM7 63412-2* ⚠

    Rec. March 1957   HMV ALP-1862; ASD-432   Ang. 35865; S-35865
    Abbey Road   HMV HQS-1136*   (tape) Ang. ZS-35865

A-313 BERLIOZ: Le Corsaire: Overture, Op. 21   *CDM7 63407-2*   ⚠

    Rec. Nov. 1958   HMV ALP-1846; ASD-420   Cap. G-7251; SG-7251
    Abbey Road.   HMV HQS-1136*   Sera. 60084; S-60084
                        HMV SXLP-30158*   Pickwick SPC-4035*
                    in HMV ALP 1870/1   in Ang. 3621B

A-314 BERLIOZ: The Damnation of Faust: Dance of the Sylphs   *CDM7 63412-2*   ⚠
    Rec. March 1957 *Abbey Road.* HMV ALP-1533; ASD-259   Ang. 35506; S-35506

A-315 BERLIOZ: Symphonie Fantastique, Op. 14   *CDM7 64032-2*   ⚠
      (R.T.F. Orchestra)

    Mono rec. Nov. 1957 ⚠   HMV ALP-1633; ASD-399   Cap. G-7102
    Stereo rec. Oct & Nov. 1959 *Salle Wagram.*   Sera. S-60165*

A- 316 BERLIOZ: Les Troyens: Marche Troyenne   *CDM7 63412-2*   ⚠
    Rec. Nov. 1959   HMV ALP-1862; ASD-432   Ang. 35865; S-35865
    Abbey Road   WRC CSJT-744*   Sera. S-60134*[3]
                                   (tape) Ang. ZS-35865

----

[1]All recordings made in stereo unless otherwise noted. Where monaural editions
existed of the same recording, stereo numbers are shown after the monaural. When
recordings were likely issued in stereo only, an asterisk follows the number.

[2]It has not been possible to determine which of the early Seraphim reissues were
released in stereo only. Capitol records (the distributor) states that all were
stereo only, however information on some jackets would seem to belie that fact.
Numbers below 60100 have been given mono equivalents, which may or may not exist.

[3]Recording date in liner note erroneous.

EMI Recordings, 1955-1959

A-317 BERLIOZ: Les Troyens: Royal Hunt and Storm Δ

    Rec. March 1957   HMV ALP-1553; ASD-259   Ang. 35506; S-35506
    Abbey Road

A-318 BIZET: L'Arlesienne: Suites Nos. 1 and 2   *CDC7 47794-2* Δ

    Rec. Sept. 1956   HMV ALP-1497; ASD-252   Ang. 35460
    Abbey Road   HMV HQS-1108*

A-319 BIZET: Carmen: Orchestral Suite (R.T.F. Orchestra)

    Rec. Nov. 1957   HMV ALP-1843
    Salle Wagram

A-320 BIZET: Carmen: Orchestral Suite (R.T.F. Orchestra)   *CDM7 63379-2* Δ

    Rec. June 1958   HMV HQS-1108*[1]   Sera. S-60134*
    Salle Wagram

A-321 BIZET: Carmen
        (Victoria de Los Angeles, Monique Linval, Denise Monteil, Nicolai
        Gedda, Janine Micheau, Marcelle Crosier, Ernest Blanc, R.T.F.
        Orchestra and Chorus)

    Rec. January 1958[3]   HMV ALP-1762/4; ASD-331/3 Ang. 3613C/L; S-3613C/L
    Salle Wagram   HMV SLS-755*   (tape) Ang.ZC-3613

                       Highlights:
                  HMV ALP-2041; ASD-590   Ang. 35818; S-35818
       (Chanson Boheme) in HMV ALP 1870/1   & in Ang. 3621B

A-322 BIZET: Patrie Overture   *CDM7 63401-2* Δ

    Rec. in mono Oct. 1956   HMV ALP-1497   Ang. 35460
    Abbey Road.   HMV HQM-1162

A-323 BIZET: Roma Ballet: Carnival   *CDM7 63401-2* Δ

    Rec. Oct. 1957   HMV ALP-1656
    Salle Wagram   HMV HQM-1162

A-324 (a) BIZET: Symphony in C major (R.T.F. Orchestra) *CDC7 47794-2* Δ
      (b) LALO: Symphony in G major   *CDM7 63395-2* Δ

    (a) Mono rec. Jan. 1958 HMV ALP-1761; ASD-388 Cap. G-7237; SG-7237[2]
        Stereo rec. Oct. &   Sera. S-60192*
        Nov. 1959
    (b) Mono rec. June 1958
        Stereo rec. Dec. 1959   *Salle Wagram*

A-325 BORODIN: Prince Igor: Polovtsian Dances   *CDC 7 47717-2* Δ
      (Beecham Choral Society, Denis Vaughan, dir.)

    Rec. Nov. 1956   HMV SXLP-30171*
    Abbey Road

A-326 BRAHMS: Academic Festival Overture, Op. 80 Δ

    Rec. Nov. 1956   Col. CX-1429   Ang. 35400; S-35400
                     HMV HQS-1143*   Sera. 60083; S-60083
                     HMV SXLP-30158*

----

[1]Beecham Society member JH has supplied reviews of this and the previous ALP-1843
which seem to indicate that there were two different recordings of the suite, and
neither were taken from the complete recording.

[2]In this instance and that of others where there is a mono equivalent of a stereo
release, there having been separate mono and stereo recordings, we have not been
able to determine if the mono is the same performance as the stereo or the earlier
mono recording. Perhaps some member who has all the pressings would undertake
the task.

[3]WB indicates that this recording may have been completed later than this date;
De Los Angeles walked out after part of the recording was finished and it was
not completed at this time.

48

EMI Recordings, 1955-1959

A-327 BRAHMS: Song of Destiny, Op. 54
          (Beecham Choral Society, Denis Vaughan, dir.)

      Rec. May & Nov. 1956   Col. CX-1429   Ang. 35400; S-35400
      Abbey Road.

A-328 BRAHMS: Symphony No. 2 in D, Op. 73[1]   △

      Rec. May & Sept.1956,   HMV ALP-1770; ASD-348 Cap. G-7228; SG-7228
      Apr,Nov.&Dec. 1958   HMV HQS-1143*   Sera. 60083; S-60083
      May,Jul,Aug.& Nov.1959
      Abbey Road.

A-329 CHABRIER: Gwendoline Overture (R.T.F. Orchestra)   *CDM7 63401-2*   △

      Rec. Nov. 1957   HMV ALP-1843
      Salle Wagram   HMV HQM-1162

A-330 CHABRIER: Marche Joyeuse   *CDM7 63412-2*   △

      Rec. March 1957
      Abbey Road.   HMV ALP-1533; ASD-259 Ang. 35506; S-35506

A-331 DEBUSSY: L'Enfant Prodigue: Cortege and Air de danse   *CDM7 63412-2* △

      Rec. Oct. & Nov. 1959   HMV ALP-1862; ASD-432 Ang. 35865; S-35865
      Abbey Road.   WRC T-558; ST-558   Sera. 60084; S-60084
                                              (tape) Ang. ZS-35865

A-332 DEBUSSY: Prelude to the Afternoon of a Faun   *CDM7 63379-2*   △

      Rec. March 1957   HMV ALP-1533; ASD-259 Ang. 35506; S-35506
      Abbey Road

A-333 DELIBES: Le Roi s'amuse: Ballet Suite   *CDM7 63379-2*   △

      Rec. May 1958   HMV ALP-1656   Sera. 60084; S-60084
      Salle Wagram   HMV HQS-1136*

A-334 DELIUS: Works for Orchestra   *CDS7 47509-8*   △
          (a) On Hearing the First Cuckoo in Spring Rec. Oct. 1956
          (b) Brigg Fair   Rec. Oct. 1956 & May 1957
          (c) A song before sunrise   Rec. Nov. 1956
          (d) Sleigh Ride   Rec. Nov. 1956
          (e) Summer Night on the River   Rec. March 1957
          (f) Marche Caprice   Rec. Oct. 1956
          (g) Intermezzo from "Fennimore & Gerda"   Rec. Nov. 1956
          Abbey Road.
                                 HMV ALP-1586; ASD-357 Cap. G-7116; SG-7116
                                                         Sera. S-60185*
                                              (a) in Sera. S-60134*

A-335 DELIUS: Works for Orchestra   *CDS7 47509-8*   △
          (a) Florida Suite   Rec. Nov. & Dec. 1956
          (b) Over the Hills and Far Away Rec. Apr. & Oct. 1957
          (c) Dance Rhapsody No. 2   Rec. Nov. 1956
          Abbey Road.
                                 HMV ALP-1697; ASD-329 Cap. G-7193; SG-7193
                                 HMV HQS-1126*   Sera. S-60212*

A-336 DELIUS: Prelude to "Irmelin"   *CDS7 47509-8*   △

      Rec. Oct. 1956   HMV ALP-1968; ASD-518 Sera. 60000; S-60000
      Abbey Road.   WRC T-744; ST-744

---

[1]Due to the disparity in recording dates it is possible that one or another of
the issues are different recordings.

EMI Recordings, 1955-1959

A-337 DELIUS: Songs of Sunset[1]   CDS7 47509-8   △
    (John Cameron, bar., Maureen Forrester, con.; Beecham Choral Society,
    Denis Vaughan, dir.)

    Rec. April 1957   HMV ALP-1983
    Abbey Road

A-338 DELIUS: Summer Evening   CDS7 47509-8   △

    Rec. Oct. 1956   HMV ALP-1968; ASD-518   Sera. 60000; S-60000
    Abbey Road

A-339 DVORAK: Legend No. 3 in G, Op. 59   CDM7 63412-2   △

    Rec. Nov. 1959   HMV ALP-1968; ASD-518   Sera. 60000; S-60000
    Abbey Road   WRC T-744; ST-744

A-340 DVORAK: Symphony No. 8 in G, Op. 88   R. Fes. Hall.

    Rec. Oct. 25, 1959 at a   HMV ALP-2003
    public concert in R.F.H., BBCTS M(S) 120
    London

A-341 FAURE: Dolly Suite (Arr. Rabaud) (R.T.F. Orchestra) CDM7 63379-2 △

    Rec. December 1959[2]   HMV ALP-1843   Sera. 60084; S-60084
    HMV HQS-1136*

A-342 FAURE: Pavane, Op. 50   (R.T.F. Orchestra)   CDM7 63379-2 △

    Rec. December 1959   HMV ALP-1968; ASD-518   Sera. 60000; S-60000
    HMV HQS-1136*   Sera. S-60134*

A-343 FRANCK: Symphony in D minor   (R.T.F. Orchestra)   CDM7 63395-2 △

    Mono rec. Nov. 1957   HMV ALP-1686; ASD-458   Cap. G-7157
    Stereo rec. Dec. 1959 WRC T-596; ST-596   Sera. 60012; S-60012
    Salle Wagram

A-344 GERMAN: Gipsy Suite   △

    Rec. Oct. 1956   HMV ALP-1983
    Abbey Road.   WRC T-558; ST-558

A-345 GOUNOD: Faust: Ballet Music   CDM7 63401-2   △

    Rec. Oct. & Nov. 1957   HMV ALP-1656
    Salle Wagram   HMV HQM-1162

A-346 GOUNOD: Romeo and Juliet: Juliet's Sleep   CDM7 63412-2   △

    Rec. Oct. & Nov. 1959   HMV ALP-1862; ASD-432 Ang. 35865; S-35865
    Abbey Road.   Sera. 60084; S-60084
                                                  (tape) Ang. ZS-35865

A-347 GRETRY: Zemire et Azor: Ballet Suite   CDM7 63401-2   △

    Rec. Oct. 1956   HMV ALP-1656
    Abbey Road.   HMV HQM-1162
    (Air de Ballet) in HMV ALP-1870/1 & Ang. 3621B

A-348 (a) GRIEG: In Autumn: Concert Overture, Op. 11   CDM7 69039-2 △
    (b) GRIEG: Old Norwegian Romance with Variations, Op. 31

    Both rec. in mono Nov.1955 Col. CX-1363   Ang. 35339
    Abbey Road.   HMV XLP-30028
    (a) in Stereo   Encore ENC-108
----
[1] Acc. to DV this recording was not approved by Beecham because the hushed manner
which he had used to illustrate the phrasing had been transmitted by Vaughan
to the soloists and chorus, who therefore tend to sing with half voice, weakening
the total effect of the work. Funds were insufficient to correct this fault
in the short studio time available.
[2] Beecham's last recording.

EMI Recordings, 1955-1959

A-349 GRIEG: Peer Gynt, Op. 23: Excerpts .... CDM7 69039-2 △
    (Judith Hollweg, sop.; Beecham Choral Society, Denis Vaughan, dir.)
Ilse
    Rec. Nov. 1956,   HMV ALP-1530; ASD-258   Ang. 35445; S-35445
      Mar. & Apr. 1957 (tape) HMV SAT-1018
Abbey Road (Arabian Dance) in HMV ALP 1870/1 & Ang. 3621B

A-350 GRIEG: Symphonic Dance, Op. 64, No. 2   CDM7 69039-2 △
    Rec. Nov. 1959   HMV ALP-1968; ASD-518 Sera. 60000; S-60000
Abbey Road.   WRC T-744; ST-744

A-351 HANDEL: Amaryllis Suite: Gavotte & Scherzo
    Rec. Oct. 1958   HMV ALP-1912; ASD-480
Kingsway Hall.   WRC T-837; ST-837

A-352 HANDEL: The Gods go a'Begging (Arr. Beecham)[1]
    Rec. April 1958   HMV ALP-1912; ASD-480
Abbey Road.   WRC T-837; ST-837

A-353 HANDEL: Love in Bath (Ballet, Arr. Beecham)[2] (w/Ilse Hollweg, soprano)
    Rec. Nov. & Dec.1956,   HMV ALP-1729; ASD-298 Ang. 35504; S-35504
      Mar,Apr. 1957,   WRC T-632; ST-632   Sera. 60039; S-60039
      Aug. & Nov. 1959   HMV SXLP-30156*   *Abbey Road.*

A-354 HANDEL: Messiah[3] (J.Vyvyan, M. Sinclair, J. Vickers, G. Tozzi, RPO Chorus)
    Rec. in London,   RCA RE-25002/5; SER 4501/4 Vic. LD-6409; LDS-6409
      Jun.6 & Jul.3, 1959, RCA SER 6531/4 [4] (excerpts) Vic. LD-2447; LDS-2447
      Aug. 17 & 18, 1959

A-355 HANDEL: Solomon[5]   △
    (J. Cameron, A. Young, E. Morison, L. Marshall, Beecham Choral Society,
     Denis Vaughan, dir.)
    Rec. Nov.& Dec. 1955,   Col. CX-1307/8; SAX 2499/500 Ang. 3546B; S-3546B
      Jan.& May 1956   WRC T-82/3; ST-82/3   Sera. SIB-6039*
Abbey Road.
               (Entrance of the Queen of Sheba only)
               HMV ALP-1912; ASD-480   Sera. S-60134*
               WRC T-837; ST-837

A-356 HAYDN: The Seasons[6]   △
    (E. Morison, A. Young, M. Langdon, Beecham Choral Society, Denis
     Vaughan, dir.)
    Rec. Nov.1956 & Mar.1957 HMV ALP-1606/8; ASD 282/4 Cap. GCR-7184; SGCR-7184
Salle Wagram.   WRC ST-786/8*

----

[1] Containing nine of the eleven movements in the complete ballet.

[2] Again, due to the disparity in recording dates one or another of the issues are probably different recordings. A member has noticed differences in orchestration between the Angel and Seraphim issues. A reworking of material originally used in "The Great Elopement" and "Origin of Design."

[3] According to WB, Beecham re-did the orchestration after he disregarded that of Sir Eugene Goossens, which was commissioned for the recording.

[4] Possibly SER 5631/4.

[5] Reorchestrated by Beecham. Omits some sections and transfers others.

[6] Omits two lines only.

EMI Recordings, 1955-1959

A-357 HAYDN: "Salomon" Symphonies, Volume 1[1]   △
    (a) Symphony No. 93 in D
        Rec. Oct. 1957   HMV ALP-1624/6   Ang. 36242/4; S-36242/4
    (b) Symphony No. 94 in G   HMV SLS-846*   Cap. GCR-7127;DGCR-7127
        Rec. Oct. 1957 &   (b)(d) HMV HQM-1148 (tape) Ang. Y3S-3658(3.75 IPS)
        Apr. 1958
    (c) Symphony No. 95 in C   *Salle Wagram*
        Rec. Oct. 1957
    (d) Symphony No. 96 in D
        Rec. Oct.&Nov. 1957;
        April 1958
    (e) Symphony No. 97 in C
        Rec. Mar. 1957 &
        April 1958
    (f) Symphony No. 98 in B-flat
        Rec. Oct.&Nov. 1957;
        April 1958

A-358 HAYDN: "Salomon" Symphonies, Volume 2[2]   *CMS7 64066-2*   △
    (a) Symphony No. 99 in E-flat
        Rec. May & Dec.1958; HMV ALP-1693/5;   Ang. 36254/6; S-36254/6
        May 1959   ASD 339/41   Cap. GCR-7198;SGCR-7198
    (b) Symphony No. 100 in G HMV SLS-846*   (tape) Ang. Y3S-3659(3.75 IPS)
        Rec. May & Dec. 1958   (b) Finale only
    (c) Symphony No. 101 in D   in HMV ALP 1870/1 & Ang. 3621B
        Rec. May & Dec. 1958;
        May 1959
    (d) Symphony No. 102 in B-flat *Abbey Road and*
        Rec. May & Dec. 1958; *Salle Wagram*
        May 1959
    (e) Symphony No. 103 in E-flat
        Rec. May & Dec. 1958;
        May 1959
    (f) Symphony No. 104 in D
        Rec. May & Dec. 1958;
        May 1959

A-359 (a) LISZT: A Faust Symphony   *CDM7 63371-2*   △
      (Alexander Young, tenor; Beecham Choral Society, Denis Vaughan, dir.)
    (b) LISZT: Orpheus   *CDM7 63299-2*   △

    (a) Rec. April & Oct. 1958 HMV ALP-1737/8;   Cap. GBR-7197;SGBR-7197
    (b) Rec. April 1958   ASD-317/18   Sera. IB-6017; SIB-6017
       Kingsway Hall.   WRC CM-78/9; SCM 78/9

A-360 LISZT: Psalm XIII   *CDM7 63299-2*   △
    (Walter Midgley, tenor; Beecham Choral Society, Denis Vaughan, dir.)

    Rec. December 1955   Col. CX-1429   Ang. 35400; S-35400
       Abbey Road.   WRC T-909; ST-909

A-361 MASSENET: Cendrillon: Valse   *CDM7 63401-2*   △

    Rec. Oct. 1957   HMV ALP-1656
       Salle Wagram   HMV HQM-1167

A-362 MENDELSSOHN: A Midsummer Night's Dream: Overture *CDM7 63407-2*   △

    Rec. Nov. 1958   HMV ALP-1846; ASD-420 Cap. G-7251; SG-7251
       Abbey Road.   WRC T-558; ST-558   Pickwick SPC-4035*
                   HMV SXLP-30158*

----

[1]Recorded in mono; stereo versions electronically produced. (a) and (c) recorded in Salle Wagram, Paris; (e) recorded in Abbey Road Studio #1, London; remainder recorded both in Paris and London.

[2]All recorded both in Salle Wagram (Paris) and Abbey Road Studio No. 1 (London).

EMI Recordings, 1955-1959

A-363 MENDELSSOHN: Fair Melusine: Overture   CDM7 63407-2   △

     Rec. Nov. 1958   HMV ALP-1846; <u>ASD-420</u>   Cap. G-7251; SG-7251
       Abbey Road,   Pickwick SPC-4035*

                                        CDM

A-364 (a) MOZART: Concerto for Clarinet & Orchestra, K. 622 (Jack Brymer, cl.)   △
      (b) MOZART: Concerto for Bassoon & Orchestra, K. 191 (Gwydion Brooke, bs.)

     (a) Rec. May 1958 & May 1959   HMV ALP-1768; ASD-344   Cap. G-7201; SG-7201
     (b) Rec. December 1958   Abbey Road.   Sera. S-60193*

A-365 (a) MOZART: Divertimento No. 2 in D, K. 131   △
     (b) MOZART: Symphony No. 41 in C, K. 551   <u>CDM7 69811-2</u>   △

     (a) Rec. in mono Dec. 1955   HMV ALP-1536   Ang. 35459
        & May 1956 and stereo   HMV HQM-1117
     (b) Rec. in mono Mar. 1957   Abbey Road
        and stereo

A-366 MOZART: The Abduction from the Seraglio, K. 384   △
        (L. Marshall, I. Hollweg, L. Simoneau, G. Unger, G. Frick, Beecham
        Choral Society, Denis Vaughan, dir.; H. Laubenthal, speaker)

      Rec. May 1956   Col. CX-1462/3; SAX 2427/9   Ang. 3555B/L; S-3555B/L
                        (tape)Col. BTA 119/21
                        HMV HQM-1050/1; HQS-1050/1
     Kingsway Hall.   <u>HMV SLS-773*</u>
             (Overture) HMV ALP-1912; ASD-480
                  "   WRC T-837; ST-837
              (Aria)in HMV C147-30636M/37
        (Rehearsal exc.) HMV EMPS-75

A-367 MOZART: March in D, K. 249   CDM7 63412-2   △

      Rec. March 1957   HMV ALP-1533; ASD-259   Ang. 35506; S-35506
       Abbey Road

A-368 MOZART: Thamos, King of Egypt, K. 345: Entr'acte No. 2   CDM7 63412-2   △

      Rec. Mar.& Apr. 1957   HMV ALP-1862; ASD-432   Ang. 35865; S-35865
       Abbey Road.   WRC T-558; <u>ST-558</u>   (tape) Ang. ZS-35865

A-369 PUCCINI: La Boheme   △
        (J. Bjoerling, R. Merrill, J. Reardon, G. Tozzi, F. Corena, V. de los
        Angeles, L. Amara, W. Nahr, T. Powell, G. Del Monte, RCA Victor
        Orchestra and Chorus, the Columbus Boychoir)

      Rec. at Manhattan Center,   HMV ALP-1409/10   Vic. LM-6042
      New York, 3/16,17,30,   <u>HMV SLS-896</u>[1]   Sera. IB-6000
      4/1,2,3,5,6, 1956   (exc.,with introductory comment
                                      by Beecham)
                                    Vic. SRL-12-28

A-370 RIMSKY-KORSAKOV: Scheherazade, Op. 35   CDC7 47717-2   △

      Rec. March 1957   HMV ALP-1564; ASD-251   Ang. 35505; S-35505
       Abbey Road.   (tape)HMV SAT-1021   (tape)Ang. ZS-35505

A-371 ROSSINI: La Cambiale di Matrimonio: Overture   CDM7 63407-2   △

      Rec. Nov. 1958 &   HMV ALP-1846; ASD-420   Cap. G-7251; SG-7251
        Nov. 1959   WRC T-558; ST-558   Pickwick SPC-4035*
        Abbey Road

----

[1]This was rumored to have been recorded experimentally in stereo. The recent HMV reissue in said in the liner note to be electronic stereo, however HMV's advertising states it was "newly remastered from the original multi-channel tapes," and according to Brian Crimp of EMI the voices were recorded on one channel, the orchestra on another, and they have apparently been mixed together with the orchestra spread out behind the voices for the new SLS reissue. Acc. to WB who was present at the session, it was recorded in stereo on a Magnavox with staggered heads.

A-372 ROSSINI: La Gazza Ladra: Overture   CDM7 63407-2   △

     Rec. Nov. 1958   HMV ALP-1846; ASD-420   Cap. G-7251; SG-7251
       Abbey Road.   WRC T-744; ST-744   Pickwick SPC-4035*
                    HMV SXLP-30158*   Sera. S-60134*

A-373 ROSSINI: Semiramide: Overture   CDM7 63407-2   ▲

     Rec. Nov. 1958   HMV ALP-1912; ASD-480
       Abbey Road.   WRC T-837; ST-837

A-374 SAINT-SAENS: Samson & Delilah: Dance of the Priestesses and Bacchanale   △
                                       CDM7 63412-2
     Rec. Oct. 1958 &   HMV ALP-1862; ASD-432   Ang. 35865; S-35865
       Nov. 1959   HMV HQS-1136*   Sera. 60084; S-60084
       Abbey Road.   (tape) Ang. ZS-35865

A-375 SAINT-SAENS: Omphale's Spinning Wheel   CDM 7 63379-2   △

     Rec. March 1957   HMV ALP-1533; ASD-259   Ang. 35506; S-35506
       Abbey Road

A-376 (a) SCHUBERT: Symphony No. 3 in D, D.200   CDM7 69750-2   △
      (b) SCHUBERT: Symphony No. 5 in B-flat, D.485   CDM7 69750-2   △

     (a) Rec. May 1958 &   *S.W*   HMV ALP-1743; ASD-345   Cap. G-7212; SG-7212
         May 1959   *A.R*
     (b) Rec. May 1958   *S.W.*   *18 Dec 1958 A.R.*

A-377 SCHUBERT: Symphony No. 6 in C, D.589   CDM7 69750-2   △

     Rec. in mono Nov. &   Col. CX-1363   Ang. 35339
       Dec. 1955   HMV XLP-30028
       Abbey Rd.   WRC T-909   *ST909: - Rec. 25-26 Nov. 1955.*
                     Encore ENC-108

A-378 SIBELIUS: Kuolema, Op. 44: Valse Triste   CDM7 63412-2   /△

     Rec. March 1957   HMV ALP-1533; ASD-259   Ang. 35506; S-35506
                                  Sera. S-60134*

A-379 (a) SIBELIUS: Oceanides, Op. 73   ⎫   CDM7 63400-2   △
      (b) SIBELIUS: Pelleas et Melisande, Op. 73[1] ⎬   △
      (c) SIBELIUS: Symphony No. 7   ⎭   △

     (a) Rec. Dec. 1955   HMV ALP-1480; ASD-468   Ang. 35458; S-35458
     (b) Rec. Nov. & Dec. 1955   (b) HMV (tape) SBT-1255 (c) Ang. (tape) ST-1002
     (c) Rec. Nov. 1955   (c) HMV (tape) SBT-1252
       Abbey Road.

A-380 SIBELIUS: Symphony No. 2 in D, Op. 43   △

     Rec. Dec. 8, 1954 at a   HMV ALP-1947
       performance in R.F.H.,   WRC ST-1085[2]
       London   BBCTS 83357/61
                        BBC Concert Hall #63

A-381 SIBELIUS: Tapiola, Op. 112   CDM7 63400-2   △

     Rec. Dec. 1955   HMV ALP-1968; ASD-518   Sera. 60000; S-60000
       Abbey Road   WRC T-744; ST-744

----

[1] Movements recorded: At the Castle Gate, Melisande, A Spring in the Park, The
Three Blind Sisters, Pastorale, Melisande at the Spinning Wheel, Entr'acte
[2] Electronic stereo

EMI Recordings, 1955-1959

A-382 STRAUSS: Ein Heldenleben, Op. 40   CDM7 63299-2 △

    Rec. April 1958   HMV ALP-1847; ASD-421   Cap. G-7250; SG-7250
    Kingsway Hall   WRC T-664; ST-664   Sera. 60041; S-60041

A-383 SUPPÉ: Poet and Peasant Overture   CDM7 63407-2 △

    Rec. March 1957   HMV ALP-1533; ASD-259   Ang. 35506; S-35506
    Abbey Road.   HMV SXLP-30158*

A-384 TCHAIKOVSKY: Eugene Onegin: Waltz   CDM7 63412-2 △

    Rec. Oct. & Nov. 1959   HMV ALP-1862; ASD-432   Ang. 35865; S-35865
    Abbey Road?   HMV HQM-1167   Sera. S-60134*
                                               (tape) Ang. ZS-35865

A-385 TCHAIKOVSKY: Symphony No. 4 in F, Op. 36   CDM7 63380-2 △

    Rec. Oct. & Nov. 1957, *S.W* HMV ALP-1667   Cap. G-7139
        April 1958 *K.H*   HMV HQM-1167   Pickwick SPC-4033*[1]
Portions survive   (Scherzo) in HMV ALP 1870/1   &   Ang. 3621B
in Stereo

A-386 VIDAL: Zino-Zina: Four Ancient Dances: Gavotte   CDM7 63412-2 △

    Rec. Oct. 1957   HMV ALP-1983
    Salle Wagram   WRC T-558; ST-558

A-387 WAGNER: Die Meistersinger: Prelude to Act 1   CDM7 63407-2 △

    Rec. Nov. 4, 1959 at a   HMV ALP-2003
    concert in R.F.H.,
    London

END OF EMI LISTING

---

[1]Electronic stereo. May not have been recorded in true stereo.

EXISTING RECORDINGS ON FILM, TAPE & DISC OF CONCERT PERFORMANCES, TALKS, ETC.

Part 1: Recordings of Concerts[1]

1936

B-1   WAGNER: Die Götterdämmerung
            (F. Lieder, H. Janssen, L. Melchior, E. List, K. Thorborg, Covent
            Garden Chorus and Orchestra) Rec. May 14, 1936

                Excerpts on EJS-167, including Act 1: Waltraute Scene
                                              Act 2: Final Scene

B-2   (a) DVORAK: Symphony in F major, Op. 76 (Old No. 3)
        (b) BEETHOVEN: Symphony No. 7 in A, Op. 92 (Intro to 1st movement only)
            (London Philharmonic Orchestra, Queens Hall, Oct. 15, 1936)

B-3   MOZART: Symphony No. 39 in E-flat, K. 543: Minuet[2]
            (London Philharmonic Orchestra; recorded on tape in Ludwigshafen,
            Germany by BASF on Nov. 19, 1936)

                Released on Hi-Fi Cassette by BASF; portion on 33 1/3 RPM
                7" disc produced by Audio Magazine

1937

B-4   (arr. Beecham) GOD SAVE THE KING
            (London Philharmonic Orchestra, LPO Chorus, Eva Turner, soprano;
            with audience participation, recorded April 1, 1937)

B-5   VAUGHAN-WILLIAMS: Flourish for a Coronation
            (London Philharmonic Orchestra & Chorus, recorded April 1, 1937)

B-6   WAGNER: Tristan and Isolde
            (K. Flagstad, L. Melchior, M. Klose, H. Janssen and others, London
            Philharmonic Orchestra) Rec. at Covent Garden, June 18, 1937

                Excerpts include: (a) Act 1 (portions of the prelude are reputedly
                                           from another recording)
                                   (b) Act 2: Fragment from beginning and end only
                                   (c) Act 3: Prelude

                                        (c) in WSA 506/7

B-7   (a) DELIUS: Dance Rhapsody No. 1: portion only
        (b) ELGAR: Introduction and Allegro: incomplete
            (London Philharmonic Orchestra, Nov. 18, 1937)

1939

B-8   BLOCH: Concerto for Violin & Orchestra [3]
            (Joseph Szigeti, violin; London Philharmonic Orchestra)
            Recorded at Queen's Hall, March 9, 1939
                                        in WSA 5 (SM)

----

[1] Arranged in approximate chronological sequence where date is known; if exact
date is unknown period is estimated.

[2] At least one other movement is in existence and has been heard by SHM.

[3] Beecham Society tape is missing music at several side breaks of 78RPM acetate
originals; those sections interpolated from commercial recording of Szigeti
and Munch for release on WSA 5 (SM).

<u>1941</u>

B-9   COLUMBIA (CBS) SYMPHONY, June 27, 1941
            (a) National Anthem[1]
            (b) Boccherini: Symphony No. 3, Op. 12
            (c) Debussy: L'Enfant Prodigue: Cortege & Air de Danse
            (d) Delius: Piano Concerto (Betty Humby, piano)
            (e) Dvorak: The Golden Spinning Wheel[2]
                Recorded over WABC, New York, 3-4 PM

                                        (Boccherini only) in WSA 520

B-10   COLUMBIA (CBS) SYMPHONY, Sept. 21, 1941[3]
            (a) Mendelssohn: Hebrides Overture
            (b) Brahms: Alto Rhapsody
            (c) Handel-Beecham: "Suite for Orchestra"
            (d) Delius: Sea Drift
                (with Members of Schola Cantorum; Janet Busch, alto; Ralph
                Nicolson, baritone)
                Recorded over WABC, 3-4:30 PM

B-11   PHILADELPHIA Orchestra, Academy of Music, Nov. 27, 1941
            (a) Haydn: Symphony No. 93[4]
            (b) Mozart: Symphony No. 41
            (c) Virgil Thomson: Symphony No. 2
            (d) Rossini: La Gazza Ladra: Overture

B- 12 "FORD" (DETROIT) Symphony Orchestra, December 28, 1941
            Tchaikovsky: Jeanne d'Arc: Adieu, forêts (Rise Stevens, soprano)

<u>1942</u>

B- 13 BIZET: Carmen
            (L. Djanel, L. Albanese, C. Kullman, L. Warren, Metropolitan Opera
            Chorus and Orchestra)
                Broadcast of January 24, 1942

B- 14 GOUNOD: Faust
            (C. Kullman, N. Cordon, L. Warren, L. Albanese, Metropolitan Opera
            Chorus and Orchestra)
                Broadcast of March 14, 1942[5]

B- 15 "FORD" (DETROIT) Symphony Orchestra, June 11, 1942
            (a) Delius: La Calinda
            (b) Debussy: Petite Suite: En Bateau
            (c) Duparc: Chanson Triste
            (d) Meyerbeer: Dinorah: Shadow Song
            (e) Thomas: Je suis Titania, from Mignon
                ⌊Items (c)(d) and (e) with Lily Pons, soprano⌉
            (f) Respighi: "Rossiniana" Suite (unspec. excerpts)
                Concert Introduced by Lionel Barrymore
                                        AFRS Concert Hall 189 and 227[6]

----

[1]Not recorded

[2]This work was scheduled, but not played due to a pre-emption by a Winston
Churchill talk.

[3]The Brahms is known to exist; the remainder of the program is catalogued in a
private collection and its existence is undetermined.

[4]First movement conducted by Saul Caston when Beecham was late in arriving.

[5]Not in Society archive, however all Met broadcasts of this period recorded by
AFRS.

[6]Recorded for Veterans Administration; transcriptions may be in existence.
AFRS discs contain Tarantella only from (f).

Recordings of Concerts

1943

B-16   MASSENET: Manon
        (B. Sayao, F. Greer, N. Moscona, C. Kullman, N. Cordon, L. Browning,
        M. Stellman, Metropolitan Opera Chorus & Orchestra)

                Broadcast of January 16, 1943

B-17   GOUNOD: Faust
        (R. Jobin, E. Pinza, J.C. Thomas, L. Albanese, W. Engelman,
        Metropolitan Opera Chorus & Orchestra)

                Broadcast of January 30, 1943   Highlights in EJS-265

B-18   CHARPENTIER: Louise
        (G. Moore, R. Jobin, D. Doe, E. Pinza, M. Stellman, Metropolitan
        Opera Chorus & Orchestra)

                Broadcast of February 20, 1943   in EJS-164

B-19   LOS ANGELES PHILHARMONIC Orchestra, August 8, 1943
        (a) Bizet: Carmen Suite
        (b) Elgar: Serenade for Strings
        (c) Humperdinck: Hansel & Gretel Overture
        (d) Popper: Hungarian Rhapsody (Lauri Kennedy, cello)
        (e) Sibelius: Karelia: March
        (f) Sibelius: Pelleas & Melisande: No. 2: Melisande
        (g) Sibelius: Valse Triste

                Recorded in Hollywood Bowl

B-20   WAGNER: Tristan und Isolde
        (L. Melchior, H. Traubel, H. Janssen, K. Thorborg, N. Cordon,
        Metropolitan Opera Chorus & Orchestra)
                Broadcast of ~~December 11~~, 1943   Cond. E. LEINSDORF
                        February 6

B-21   THOMAS: Mignon
        (R. Stevens, P. Munsel, J. Melton, N. Cordon, A. de Paolis,
        Metropolitan Opera Chorus & Orchestra)
                Broadcast of December 25, 1943

B-22   BIZET: Carmen
        (L. Djanel, R. Jobin, L. Albanese, L. Warren, Metropolitan Opera
        Chorus and Orchestra)

                Broadcast of March 27, 1943 on tour in Chicago

1944

B-23   BIZET: Carmen
        (L. Djanel, N. Conner, T. Votipka, L. Browning, R. Jobin, A. Sved,
        Metropolitan Opera Chorus & Orchestra)

                Broadcast of January 22, 1944[1]

B-24   OFFENBACH: The Tales of Hoffmann
        (P. Munsel, L. Djanel, J. Novotna, R. Jobin, M. Harrell, E. Pinza,
        M. Singher, Metropolitan Opera Chorus & Orchestra)

                Broadcast of February 26, 1944   in IGI-324/6

B-25   VERDI: Falstaff (in English)
        (L. Warren, J. Brownlee, C. Kullman, E. Steber, J. Gurney,
        Metropolitan Opera Chorus & Orchestra)

----

[1] Not in Society archive, however all Met broadcasts of this period recorded
by AFRS.

Recordings of Concerts

B-26   GOUNOD: Faust (Metropolitan Opera)
            (Cast unknown; broadcast of a performance in Boston on tour,
            April 15, 1944; not known if was recorded)

B-27   LOS ANGELES PHILHARMONIC Orchestra, August 27, 1944
            (a) Thomas: Mignon Overture
            (b) Smetana: The Bartered Bride: Polka & Dance
            (c) Strauss: Voices of Spring
            (d) Haydn: Concerto No. 1 in D: 2nd & 3rd movements (Amparo Iturbi, pf.)
            (e) Gounod: Faust Ballet Music

1945

B-28   "FORD" (DETROIT) Symphony Orchestra, Programs ca. 1945
            Program #1: (a) Sibelius: Karelia March
                         (b) Mendelssohn: Symphony No. 3: Scherzo
                         (c) Handel: The Great Elopement: Hornpipe, Minuet & Gigue
                         (d) Rimsky-Korsakov: Antar: Oriental March
                         (e) Chabrier: Marche Joyeuse
                         (f) J. Strauss: Vienna Blood Waltz[1]
                         (g) Rimsky-Korsakov: Scheherazade: Finale[1]

            Program #2: (a) Thomas: Mignon Overture
                         (b) Suppé: Morning, Noon and Night in Vienna
                         (c) Tchaikovsky: Eugene Onegin: Waltz
                         (d) Trad: Scottish Ballad "Lord Randall"(Gilbert Russell,ten.)
                         (e) Barnby: Now the day is over   "   "
                         (f) Bizet: Carmen: March of the Smugglers
                         (g) Verdi: La Traviata: Brindisi-un di felice (with
                                    Chorus, Gilbert Russell & unidentified soprano)
                         (h) Wagner: Tristan: Liebestod

                                (a)(b)(c)(f)(h) in AFRS CX 7/9

            Program #3: (a) Overture (unid.)
                         (b) Mozart: Allelujah (Dorothy Maynor, soprano)
                         (c) Tchaikovsky: Symphony No. 5: 4th movement excerpt

B-29   "BLUE NETWORK" (A.B.C. SYMPHONY) Orchestra
            April 7: (a) Nicolai: Merry Wives of Windsor Overture
                      (b) Elgar: Serenade for Strings
                      (c) Handel: The Great Elopement: Suite of 3 movements[2]
                      (d) Delius: Village Romeo: Walk to the Paradise Garden
                      (e) Strauss: Voices of Spring   (c) in WSA 520
            April 14: (a) Mozart: Symphony No. 31
                       (b) Handel-Beecham: Piano Concerto (Betty Humby, piano)
                       (c) Chabrier: Espana
                                                          (b) in WSA 520
            April 28: (a) Berlioz: Les Troyens: Royal
                                    Hunt and Storm (Excerpt)
                       (b) Berlioz: Rakoczy March

1947

B- 30   BERLIOZ: Les Troyens
            (D. Dowling, M. Ferrer, C. Cambon, J. Giraudeau, C. Paul, et al,
            with the BBC Theatre Chorus and Royal Philharmonic Orchestra)

            Broadcasts of 3 & 6 June,   in WSA 513/16
                          2 & 4 July   EJS 377/8

----

[1]Introduced by Beecham
[2]World Premiere

Recordings of Concerts

<u>1947</u>

B-31 (a) STRAUSS: Intermezzo: Entr'acte
      (b) STRAUSS: Ariadne auf Naxos: Final Scene
          (with Maria Cebotari,sop; Carl Friederich, ten.; Royal Philharmonic)

      Recorded at Drury Lane, Oct. 12, 1947   (b) in EJS-536

B-32 STRAUSS: Elektra
          (with E. Schlütter, L. Welitsch, P. Schoeffler, W. Widdop, E. Erbach,
          Royal Philharmonic Orchestra and Chorus)

      Recorded in BBC Studio, 24 & 26 Oct.1947   in WSA 509/12
                                                      in UORC-171
                                                        Rococo 1005[1]

B-33 CHERUBINI: Le Due Journées (The Water-Carriers)
          (J. Micheau,.P. Gianotti, C. Paul, with the Bax Orchestra & Chorus)

      Recorded December 2 or 19, 1947   UORC-174
                                              (excerpts) in EJS-385

<u>1948</u>

B-34 WAGNER: Die Walküre: Excerpts
          (Konetzni, Lorenz, Bjoerck, Boehm, Wettergren, B.B.C. Symphony Orch.)

      Recorded from B.B.C.

B-35 MOZART: Thamos, King of Egypt, K. 345: Selections
          (Roger Rico, bar.; Royal Philharmonic Orchestra)

      Recorded July 5, 1948   in EJS-385

B-36 MOZART: Clemenza di Tito: Excerpts[2]
          (D. Bond, M. Ritchie, T. Anthony, Royal Philharmonic Orchestra)

      Recorded June 27, 1948   in EJS-385

<u>1950</u>

B-37 STRAUSS: Ariadne auf Naxos[3]
          (M. Thomas, M. Springer, A. Cantelo, H. Zadek, D. Craig, I. Hollweg,
          A. Young, P. Anders, M. Dickie, Royal Philharmonic Orchestra and
          Edinburgh Festival Chorus)

      Recorded August 23, 1950   in WSA 509/12

B-38 (a) DELIUS: Dance Rhapsody No. 1
      (b) BANTOCK: Fifine at the Fair   (all with Royal Philharmonic Orch.)
      (c) BRAHMS: Variations on a Theme by Haydn

          Rec. in Los Angeles, Calif. from   (c) in WSA 508
          BBC tapes, early 1950's. Beecham
          introduces each work.

B-39 (a) DELIUS: Scenes from Act 2 of Irmelin
      (b) DELIUS: Irmelin: Act 3 complete
          (with Royal Philharmonic Orch.)   16 SEP 54 RAH

      Recorded in early 1950"s. Sept 16, 1954   (a) in WSA 501
--------------------------   R.A.H.

[1]Interpolates commercial recording of last scene.
[2]Excerpts: S'alto che lagrime; De al volto.
[3]Includes Moliere play as introduction.

Recordings of Concerts

1951

B-40   WAGNER: Die Meistersinger: Acts 1 and 2
          (H. Hotter, E. Grümmer, P. Anders, M. Dickie et al, Royal Opera House
          Orchestra & Chorus, Covent Garden)
            Recorded July 2, 1951

B-41   BALFE: The Bohemian Girl: Excerpts
          (R. Peters, H. Glyene, A. Marlowe; Covent Garden Orchestra)
            Recorded August 18, 1951

1952

B-42   (a) SIBELIUS: Symphony No. 4
        (b) JOHNSTONE: Celebration Overture
          (B.B.C. Symphony Orchestra)
            Recorded ca. 1952 from BBC broadcast.

B- 43   BOSTON SYMPHONY Orchestra, January 27, 1952
          (a) Handel: The Faithful Shepherd: Suite
          (b) Sibelius: Symphony No. 6
          (c) Delius: Summer Night on the River
          (d) Delius: Marche Caprice
          (e) Rimsky-Korsakov: Le Coq d'Or: Suite

B- 44   (a) WAGNER: Wesendonck Songs
        (b) WAGNER: Tristan und Isolde: Prelude and Liebestod
          (Kirsten Flagstad, sop; Royal Philharmonic Orchestra)
            Recorded December 21, 1952 (1951?)   Liebestod from(b) in EJS-399

1954

B- 45   MOZART: Symphony No. 35
          (Bergen Festival Orchestra)
             Recorded ca. 1954; CBS "Summer Music
             Festivals" rebroadcast

B- 46   (a) RIMSKY-KORSAKOV: Le Coq d'Or: March
        (b) MASSENET: Le Vierge: Last Sleep of the Virgin   (All with R.P.O.)
        (c) SIBELIUS: Symphony No. 7[1]
          Possibly rec. in Albert Hall during
          "Proms" concerts.

B- 47   SIBELIUS: Symphony No. 6
          (Royal Philharmonic Orchestra)
            Recorded Sept. 15, 1954

B- 48   LISZT: Die Lorelei
          (Rosina Raisbeck, soprano)
            Recorded Nov. 22, 1954)   in WSA-501

B- 49   HELSINKI CITY Symphony Orchestra, Sibelius Festival, 1954
          All-Sibelius Program: Tapiola, Tempest Suite; Symphonies 6 and 7

B- 50   (a) BERLIOZ: King Lear Overture
        (b) SIBELIUS: Symphony No. 2
          (B.B.C. Symphony Orchestra)
          Recorded in R.F.H., Dec. 8, 1954   BBCTS 83357/61
                                             BBCTS Concert Hall #63
                          (a) in WSA 502/3
                          (b) in HMV ALP-1947 & WRC ST-1085

----

[1]Possibly same as B-65.

Recordings of Concerts

1955

B-51 ARNELL: Ode to the West Wind[1]
          (Jennifer Vyvyan, soprano; Royal Philharmonic Orchestra)

          Recorded February 23, 1955

B-52 SIBELIUS: Swanwhite Suite[2]
          (Royal Philharmonic Orchestra)

          Recorded December 8, 1955

B-53 (a) CHABRIER: Gwendoline Overture
       (b) GRIEG: Symphonic Dances   (All with Royal Philharmonic Orch.)
       (c) GODARD: Concerto Romantique (Alfredo Campoli, violin)

          Recorded December 25, 1955   (c) in WSA-501

1956

B-54 UNIVERSITY OF ILLINOIS Concerts, All-Mozart
          (with student soloists & University of Illinois Orchestra)
          April 24: Symphony No. 41
                     Requiem, K. 626 (in Beecham's edition)

          April 26: Divertimento in D, K. 131
                     Symphony No. 31
                     Marriage of Figaro: Act 2 (in Beecham's English translation)

B-55 (a) ELGAR (Arr.): God Save the Queen
       (b) BEETHOVEN: Symphony No. 9
          (S. Fischer, N. Merriman, R. Lewis, K. Borg, Royal Philharmonic
          Orchestra and Edinburgh Royal Choral Union)

          Recorded at Edinburgh Festival,   in WSA 504/5
          August 19, 1956   BBCTS 89569/74

B-56 BRAHMS: Symphony No. 2 in D
          (Royal Philharmonic Orchestra)

          Rec. at Edinburgh Festival,   BBCTS (Number unknown)
              August 20, 1956

B-57 (a) STRAUSS: Don Quixote (Frederick Riddle, viola; John Kennedy, cello)
       (b) BERLIOZ: Harold in Italy (Frederick Riddle, viola; both with R.P.O.)

          Rec. at Edinburgh Festival,   in WSA 506/7
              August 22, 1956   BBCTS 89588/94

B-58 BALAKIREV: Symphony No. 1 in C
          (Royal Philharmonic Orchestra)

          Recorded August 23, 1956

B-59 BIZET: Fair Maid of Perth
          (M. Dobbs, A. Pollack, A. Young, N. Miller, D. Ward, O. Brannigan,
          Royal Philharmonic Orchestra)

          Rec. October 5, 1956   in EJS-269 (Acts 1 & 2)
                                                   EJS-438 (Acts 3 & 4)

B-60 (a) MOZART: Symphony No. 29
       (b) ALWYN: Symphony No. 3[1]
          (B.B.C. Symphony Orchestra)
          Rec. at R.F.H., Oct. 10, 1956   BBCTS MTX-525
----

[1]First performance
[2]Sibelius 90th Birthday concert

62

Recordings of Concerts

1956

B-61   LISZT: A Faust Symphony
       (A. Young, ten; Beecham Choral Society; Royal Philharmonic Orchestra)
       Recorded November 14, 1956

B-62   BBC STUDIO CONCERT, October 29, 1956[1] (Royal Philharmonic Orchestra)
       (a) Chabrier: Espana Rhapsody
       (b) Debussy: L'enfant Prodigue: Cortege and Air de Danse
       (c) Mozart: Divertimento No. 2 in D, K. 131
       (d) Rimsky-Korsakov: Le Coq d'Or: Death of King Dodon
       (e) Delius: Brigg Fair
       (f) Massenet: La Vierge: Last Sleep of the Virgin

B-63   (a) SAINT-SAENS: Rouet d'Omphale
       (b) DELIUS: Dance Rhapsody No. 1[2]
       (c) STRAUSS: Der Rosenkavalier Suite (Arr. Strauss) (All with R.P.O.)
       (d) STRAUSS: Der Bürger als Edelmann Suite

       Rec. from BBC, ca. 1956

1957

B-64   SYMPHONY OF THE AIR, Carnegie Hall, New York (Portions of concerts)

       Jan. 23rd: (a) Grieg: The Last Spring[3]
                   (b) Berlioz: Les Troyens: Marche Troyenne
                   (c) Brahms: Symphony No. 3

       Jan. 27th: (d) Strauss: Dance of the 7 Veils from "Salome"
                   (e) Beethoven: Symphony No. 4

                                (a)(b)(d) in WSA-5 (SM)
                                      (c) in WSA-508
                                      (e) in WSA-504/5

1958

B-65   BBC STUDIO CONCERT, ca. 1958   (Royal Philharmonic Orchestra)
       (a) Wagner: Tannhäuser: Overture & Venusberg Music (With Chorus)
       (b) Sibelius: Symphony No. 7
       (c) Bizet: L'Arlesienne Suite No. 1: Minuet & Carillon

                                (a) in WSA-506/7
                                    BBCTS 98645/7

B-66   STRAUSS: Four Last Songs
       (Concertgebouw Orchestra of Amsterdam; Lois Marshall, soprano)
       Recorded ca. 1958.

B-67   VERDI: Otello[4]
       (R. Vinay, A. Stella, G. Taddei, I. Pasini, G. Modesti, Teatro
       Colon Orchestra & Chorus)
       Recorded July, 1958 at Teatro Colon, Argentina

B-68   BEETHOVEN: Fidelio
       (G. Brouenstein, H. Hopf, A. van Mill, P. Schoeffler, M. Dickie,
       O. Chelavine, Teatro Colon Orchestra and Chorus)
       Recorded July, 1958 at Teatro Colon, Argentina

----

[1]100th BBC "Music to Remember" program. Includes remarks by Beecham.
[2]May be same as B-73.
[3]Played as a memorial to Arturo Toscanini.
[4]Beecham's debut at Teatro Colon.

<u>1958</u>

B-69   ROYAL FESTIVAL HALL Concert, October 1958   (Royal Philharmonic Orchestra)
    (a) God Save the Queen
    (b) Schubert: Symphony No. 3   (a) Granada TV 7ess 11 (rel.1961)[1]
    (c) Mendelssohn: Symphony No. 4

      (First half only broadcast)

<u>1959</u>

B-70   CHICAGO Symphony Orchestra, Television Concerts, ca. 1959
        No. 1: Haydn: Symphony No. 102
             Mozart: Symphony No. 38

        No. 2: Mendelssohn: Fingal's Cave Overture
             Delius: "On the River" from Florida Suite
             Saint-Saens: Omphale's Spinning Wheel
             Handel-Beecham: Love in Bath

B-71   ROYAL FESTIVAL HALL Concert, Oct. 25, 1959 (Royal Philharmonic Orchestra)
    (a) Haydn: Symphony No. 101 in D
    (b) Lalo: Symphony in G minor
    (c) Dvorak: Symphony No. 8 in G, Op. 88

                         BBCTS M(S) 120
                   (c) in HMV ALP-2003

B-72   BBC STUDIO Concert, November 4, 1959   (Royal Philharmonic Orchestra)
    (a) Wagner: Die Meistersinger: Prelude to Act 1
    (b) Saint-Saens: Samson & Delilah: Dance of the Priestesses & Bacchanale
    (c) Delius: North Country Sketches
    (d) Berlioz: Les Troyens: Royal Hunt and Storm
    (e) Brahms: Symphony No. 2

             (a)(b)(c) in BBCTS Concert Hall #67
                  (a) in HMV ALP-2003

B-73   BBC STUDIO Concert, ca. 1959   (Royal Philharmonic Orchestra)
    (a) Mozart: Symphony No. 35
    (b) Delius: Dance Rhapsody No. 1
    (c) Tchaikovsky: Nutcracker Suite

                   BBCTS 100141/4

B-74   ROYAL FESTIVAL HALL Concert, November 8, 1959 (R.P.O.)
    (a) Mendelssohn: Fair Melusine Overture
    (b) Ghedini: Musica di Concierto (Frederick Riddle, viola)
    (c) Addison: Carte Blanche
    (d) Beethoven: Symphony No. 7
    (e) Saint-Saens: Samson & Delilah: Dance of the Priestesses
    (f) Debussy: L'enfant Prodigue: Cortege and Air de danse
    (g) Gounod: Romeo and Juliet: Juliet's Dream
                   BBCTS 104729/33
            (d)(e)(f)(g) in WSA-519
                (a) in WSA-508

----

[1]Not certain if this record is from this performance.

Recordings of Concerts

1958

B-75   BERLIOZ: Requiem Mass
        (R. Lewis, ten.; Royal Philharmonic Orchestra & Chorus)

        Rec. at Royal Albert Hall,   BBCTS M(S) 119
            December 13, 1958   in   WSA 502/3

1960

B-76   SEATTLE Symphony Orchestra, February 18, 1960
        (a) Berlioz: Le Corsaire Overture
        (b) Delibes: Le roi s'amuse: Ballet Suite
        (c) Gounod: Romeo & Juliet: Juliet's Dream
        (d) Gounod: Faust Ballet Music
        (e) Handel: Amaryllis Suite
        (f) Delius: Hassan: Intermezzo and Serenade
        (g) Berlioz: Les Troyens: Marche Troyenne
        (h) Saint-Saens: Samson & Delilah: Dance of the Priestesses &
                            Bacchanale

            Recorded in stereo. Includes   in WSA 517/18
            remarks by Beecham.

B- 77   TORONTO Symphony Orchestra, Television Concert, 1960
        (a) Suppé: Morning, Noon and Night in Vienna
        (b) Saint-Saens: Omphale's Spinning Wheel
        (c) Sibelius: Karelia: March
        (d) Massenet: La Vierge: Last Sleep of the Virgin
        (e) Rossini: La Gazza Ladra Overture

            Includes remarks by Beecham.

                    END OF RECORDINGS OF CONCERTS

                    ADDENDA TO PART 1

The following information was received subsequent to assembling the above:

1945

B-78   "FORD" (DETROIT) SYMPHONY Orchestra, ca. 1945[1]
        AFRS Concert Hall No. 192: (a)Wagner: Immolation Scene from
                                            "Die Götterdämmerung"
                                   (b)Trad.: La guaya
                                   (c)Trad.: The Holy City
                                   (d)Mendelssohn: Scherzo from A
                                            Midsummer Night's Dream
                                   (e)Trad.: Scotch Medley
                                   (f)Glinka: Russlan & Ludmilla Overture

                                      Items(a)(c) and (e) with Marjorie
                                      Lawrence; concert hosted by
                                      Lionel Barrymore

        AFRS Concert Hall No. 178: (a)J. Strauss: Vienna Life
                                   (b)Handel-Beecham: The Great Elopement;
                                                        Excerpts
                                   (c)Berlioz: Roman Carnival Overture
                                   (d)Bizet: Carmen: Gypsy Dance (incomplete)
                                      Concert hosted by Lionel Barrymore

        AFRS "At Ease" No. 606:   (a)J. Strauss: Treasure Waltz from
                                                    The Gypsy Baron
                                   (b)Wagner: Tristan: Isolde's Liebestod

----
[1]Recorded for Veterans Administration; transcriptions may be in existence.
These are likely "made-up" programs from several different dates; orchestra is
unnamed.

Part 2: The Films

B-79   "FOR WHOM THE GODS LOVE" (US Title: MOZART)

Released in 1934; ATP (ABFD) reissue in 1949; Director: Basil Dean
Singers include Oda Slobodskaya, Percy Hemming, Tudor Davies,
Enid James, Sylvia Nells, with Beecham conducting the L.P.O.
in arias from Marriage of Figaro and Magic Flute (Bernhard
Paumgartner conducted the remainder of the music in the film).

B-80   "THE RED SHOES"

Released in 1948; Beecham conducting the R.P.O. in the music,
danced by Moira Shearer, with Anton Walbrook and Marius Goring.
Ballet sequence released on Japanese Victor 78s in Japan (See
section IV).

B-81   "THE TALES OF HOFFMANN"

Released in 1950; Beecham conducting the R.P.O. in the music,
with singers including Owen Brannigan, Dorothy Bond, Robert
Rounseville, Margherita Grandi, Monica Sinclair. Released on
English Decca 78s and LP; reissued in America on London and Turnabout
(see Section IV).

B-82   "HONEYMOON"

Released in 1958; Beecham conducting an un-named orchestra;
recorded in Rome using multi-channel techniques. Produced and
directed by Michael Powell, with dancers Leonid Massine, Ludmila
Tcherina, and Antonio. Music includes Zapateado by Sarasate,
a substantially complete performance of Falla's El Amor Brujo,
and the Lovers of Teruel by Mikis Theoradakis. There were other
popular type musical selections that may have been conducted by
Wally Stott.

Part 3: Rehearsals

B-83   SIR THOMAS BEECHAM IN REHEARSAL

Contents: Haydn: Symphonies 100, 101, 104: rehearsal sequences
recorded in Salle Wagram, Paris, in May 1958

Mozart: The Abduction from the Seraglio: rehearsal sequences:
(a) Osmin's Aria, Act 3
(b) Osmin-Belmonte Duet, Act 1
(c) Osmin's Aria, Act 1
(d) Accompaniment to Chorus of Janissaries, Act 1
(e) Accompaniment to Constanze's Aria, Act 1
(f) Constanze's Recitative, Act 2

with Gottlob Frick, Leopold Simoneau, Lois Marshall;
Beecham Choral Society, Denis Vaughan, dir.

All with the Royal Philharmonic Orchestra, rec. summer 1956

HMV ALP-1874   High Fidelity Magazine
WRC SH-147   (Promotion record)
in HMV SLS-846

(Osmin's Aria, Act 3) in HMV EMPS-75

Part 4: <u>Talks & Lectures</u>[1]

Title	Date, if known
The London Music Festival	April 23, 1939
Delius' A Mass of Life	June 5, 1951
The Gramophone	1951
On Mozart, at Library of Congress	Nov. 19, 1949
Delius' Irmelin (as introduction to the work)	Nov. 17, 1953
Memories of the Halle Orchestra	Jan. 8, 1953
'Records I like' (~~Desert Island Discs~~)	Feb. 3, 1951
Opera in England	Aug. 3, 1951
Last Sleep of the Virgin[3]	Oct. 22, 1956
Sibelius	Nov. 24, 1955
Mozart and His Music, at Library of Congress	Feb. 6, 1956
The Changing Musical World, " " "	Feb. 25, 1957
Mozart, at University of Illinois	April 26, 1956
Mozart, at Chicago Arts Club	1956
Handel, at Chicago Arts Club	1956 (Portion on WSA 520)
Ethel Smyth	Apr. 19, 1958
about Lollipops[3]	?
Talk to Schools (80th Birthday)	Apr. 28, 1959
Tribute to Eva Turner (This is your life)	Sept. 14, 1959
Christmas Day (talks& plays LPs)	Dec. 25, 1960
Anecdotes	?
Foyles Literary Luncheon	?
on Delius to Edmund Tracy	?
"Storytelling"	?
Beecham as a disc jockey (intro. by Spike Hughes)	?
(Works played: Bartered Bride Dance;	
Marriage of Figaro Overture, etc.)	

Part 5: <u>Interviews</u>

By Martin Bookspan, WQXR, New York	January 1959
"Small World" (with Callas & Borge) by Ed Murrow	1959 (Issued on Penzance 5)
in Boston, on WGBH	January 1952
By Winifred Vaughan-Thomas	in Paris, 1959
Toronto, Spring 1960 by Ian Dougherty	1960
on Granada TV, by Peter Brook, including	?
"Lincoln's Inn" interview	
about Delius	Nov. 22, 1959

Part 6: <u>Programs about Beecham</u>

80th Birthday Tributes, by Norman del Mar,	1959
Charles Kennedy Scott, Frederick Riddle,	
Dennis Arundell, Charles Craig, Terence	
McDonagh, Jack Brymer, Felix Aphrahamian	
Announcement of Beecham's death	March 29, 1961
In Memoriam- Music magazine	1961
A Tribute to Beecham (including Leon Goossens,	May 1959[2]
Neville Cardus & Sir Malcolm Sargent)	
Beecham Society lectures (a few of those recorded)	Various dates
Anthony Griffith, Sir Neville Cardus,	
Victor Olof, Denham Ford, Richard Temple-	
Savage, David Bicknell, Stanford Robinson)	
CBC Documentary, including Vaughan-Thomas	?
interview and comments by Walter Legge	

----

[1]Excluding those remarks within concerts

[2]Issued on BBCTS T-93

[3]before encores

Part 6: Programs about Beecham (cont'd)

Title	Date, if known
Interview in Toronto of Marcel Ray, who played under Beecham, by Paul Hoeffler	?
Portrait of Beecham by Peter Heyworth	March 26, 1968
Walter Legge on Beecham, CBC 1968	1968
Eric Fenby on Beecham	?
Szigeti on Beecham: Interview by Ward Botsford	July 25, 1965
"Tommy", An affectionate portrait	?
Klaus G. Roy lectures on Beecham	?
Rabbi H.J. Hirsch comments on Beecham's "La Boheme"	June 1969
Interview about Beecham in Cleveland with Leopold Simoneau, Lois Marshall, and Jack Saul, by Ted Vietz	1967
Beecham's "March for Band," played by the Irish Guards Band	?
A Concert in Honor of Beecham, given at St. Helens, with the R.P.O. conducted by Denis Vaughan Handel-Beecham: Amaryllis Suite Mozart: Symphony No. 38 Delius: A Song Before Sunrise Bizet: Symphony in C major	March 17, 1975
A rehearsal of Beecham's arrangement of Handel: Amaryllis Suite, with Leopold Stokowski and the American Symphony Orchestra	October 1963

Part 7: Recordings rumored or alleged to exist

B-84 Brahms: Concerto No. 1 with Solomon, piano

This performance, existing on tape, is alleged to be Beecham.

B-85 Delius: Irmelin (complete)

This performance, given in 1953, is reputed to exist in part at least.

B-86 Gretry: Zemire et Azor   (complete)

A tape of this work is reputed to exist but has not been heard by the editor.

B-87 Bantock: A Pagan Symphony   (with Queen's Hall Orchestra)

This performance, listed in the discography published in LGB, is not Beecham but probably Wood or Boult.

B-88 Mozart: Symphony No. 41   (with London Philharmonic Orchestra)

Portions recorded in stereo in 1933, existing test pressings.[1]

B-89 Schubert: Symphony No. 9 in C major

Performed in late 1950's, may be existing tape[2]

B-90 Rimsky-Korsakov: Le Coq d'Or
Bach: Phoebus and Pan

Metropolitan Opera; may have been broadcast in San Francisco.[2]

B-91 Wagner: Der Ring des Nibelungen (Leider, Janssen, Melchior, Thorborg)
Strauss: Elektra (Rose Pauly)
Mozart: Don Giovanni (Pinza, Rethberg, Tauber)

Covent Garden recordings, 1938/39 season[3]

[1]Mentioned in BIRS Journal, Jan. 1967
[2]According to WB.
[3]Recorded on film, exist and have been heard by WB, who indicates that EMI was interested in issuing them but the British unions wanted their fees based on 1975 scales, not 1938, so EMI gave up.

BIBLIOGRAPHY

This listing of books and articles by and about Beecham is by no means complete, however for those who did not witness it's appearance in Sir Thomas Beecham, Conductor and Impresario by Prof. Humphrey Procter-Gregg (Westmoreland Gazette,Kendal, Westmoreland, England, 1973) we reprint it here. The above book may still be obtained by application to the publishers directly; price is $10 U.S. including postage. It is a delightful essay of anecdotes and reminiscences by many of his contemporaries and should not be missed by anyone professing an interest in him.

Other publications of note:

Thomas Beecham, A Mingled Chime, Leaves from an Autobiography. Hutchinson, 1944. (Putnam, N.Y., 1943)

Thomas Beecham, Frederick Delius. Hutchinson, 1959.

Lord (Robert) Boothby), My Yesterdays, Your Tomorrow. Hutchinson, 1962.

Adrian C. Boult, Thoughts on Conducting. Phoenix House Ltd, London, 1963.

Neville Cardus, Sir Thomas Beecham, A Memoir. Collins, 1961.

Clare Delius, Frederick Delius, Memories of My Brother. Nicholson and Watson, 1935/37.

Robert Elkin, Royal Philharmonic. Rider and Company, London, 1946.

Frederic Gaisberg, Music on Record.

Berta Geissmar, The Baton and the Jackboot. Hamish Hamilton Ltd., 1944.

Frank Howes, The English Musical Renaissance. Secker and Warburg, 1966.

Gerald Jackson, First Flute. Dent, 1968.

Michael Kennedy, The Hallé Tradition. Manchester University Press, 1960.

Ivor Newton, At the Piano. Hamish Hamilton, 1966.

Charles Reid, Beecham: An Independent Biography. Gollancz, 1961.

Harold Rosenthal, Two Centuries of Opera at Covent Garden. Putnam, 1958.

Harold Rosenthal, Opera at Covent Garden: A Short History. Victor Gollancz Ltd,1967.

Thomas Russell, Philharmonic. Hutchison, 1942.

Harold C. Schoenberg, The Great Conductors. Simon & Schuster, 1967 (Gollancz, 1968).

Bernard Shore, The Orchestra Speaks. Longmans, Green, 1938.

Ethel Smyth, Beecham and Pharoah. Chapman and Hall, 1935.

And of course we cannot neglect our own work:

Le Grand Baton, Journal of the Sir Thomas Beecham Society, published 4 times a year.
    Editor: Thomas E. Patronite
    Publisher: Stanley H. Mayes
    ---Editorial Associates---
        Nathan E. Brown
        Edwin K. Einstein Jr.
        Raymond Kolcaba
        David B. Markle
        Ralph Stone
        Bruce R. Wellek
    London Editor: Denham V. Ford
    Opera Editor: Tom Villella
    Production Design: John Froben
    Production Assistant: James J. Matzinger

Thus far (as of June 1975) eleven volumes totalling 29 issues have been published. In addition, the Society publishes a semiannual Bulletin, and a periodic Newsletter is published in England by the Chairman, Denham V. Ford.

The Society, founded in America in 1964, has a world-wide membership. For those desiring additional information, please write to one of the following addresses:

In U.S.A. and countries other than United Kingdom and Europe:
    Stanley H. Mayes, Executive Secretary
    The Sir Thomas Beecham Society
    664 South Irena Avenue
    Redondo Beach, California 90277, USA

In United Kingdom and Europe:
    Denham V. Ford, Chairman
    The Sir Thomas Beecham Society
    46, Wellington Avenue
    Westcliff-on-Sea, Essex SSO 9XB England

All numbers are A- prefix except where otherwise indicated. Where an issue was
either monaural or stereo only, prefix is shown; where no prefix is shown issue was
published in both mono and stereo. Exceptions to this rule are noted as they occur

AFRS

CX 7/9	B-28
Concert Hall 178	B-78
Concert Hall 189	B-15
Concert Hall 192	B-78
Concert Hall 227	B-15
"At Ease" 606	B-78

Angel (Ang.= mono only)

Ang. 35339	348,377
35399	308
35400	326,327,360
35445	349
35458	379
Ang. 35459	365
Ang. 35460	318,322
35504	353
35505	370
35506	314,317,330,
	332,367,375,
	378,383
35509	310
35818	321
35865	312,316,331,
	346,368,374,384
36242/4	357
36254/6	358
3546B	355
3613C/L	321
Ang. 3621B	10,48,56,58,
	93,97,105,
	124,129,173,186,
	220,226,233,313,
	321,347,349,358,385
COLC-114	39,45,46
ST-1002	379
Y3S-3658	357
Y3S-3659	358
ZC-3613	321
ZS-35505	370
ZS-35865	312,316,331,
	346,368,374,384

BBCTS

83357/61	380,B50
89569/74	B55
89588/94	B57
98645/7	B65
100141/4	B73
104729/33	B74
M(S) 119	B75
M(S) 120	340,B71
MTX-525	B60
Concert Hall #63	380,B50
Concert Hall #67	B72

Capitol (Prefix G; SG)

G-7102	315
7116	334
7127 (GCR)	357
G-7139	385
G-7157	343
7168	309
7184 (GCR)	356
7193	335

Capitol

7197 (GBR)	359
7198 (GCR)	358
7201	364
7212	376
7223	311
7228	328
7237	324
7250	382
7251	313,362,363,
	371,372

CBS

30055	271
30056	263,266
61182/3	267
61224	263,270
61271	262,264,270
61354	260,268
61431	244,254

Columbia

5132-M	45
7093-M	19
7094-M	10
7095-M	14
7123-M	42
7138/9-M	27
7145	22
7166/9-M	25
7189-M	37,38
7190-M	37
7191-M	37
7193-M	28
9077-M	105
9085/6-M	55
9092-M	32
9320/37	37
11030/6-D	62
11068/74-D	61
11137/43-D	63
11875/6-D	133
11890/2-D	132
11956/9-D	130
12902-D	70,132
17044-D	75
17050-D	89
17087-D	68
50092-D	37,38
50093-D	37
50094-D	37
50099-D	45
50100-D	39,43
50109-D	39
65018-D	19
65019-D	10
65020-D	14
67223/6-D	26
67474-D	35
67475-D	33
67661/3-D	41
68154/5-D	30
68156-D	76
68159/62S-D	82
68199/202-D	98

Columbia

68301-D	104
68339/41-D	87
68384/5-D	56
68386/7-D	70
68390/1-D	103
68402/4-D	101
68409-D	115
68412-D	74
68474/5-D	107
68590-D	114
68593/4-D	121
68600/17-D	37
68620/5-D	57
68630/2-D	80
68646-D	40
68692-D	100
68743/4-D	52
68771/4-D	102
68854-D	123
68881-D	98,107
68882-D	53
68888-D	84
68921-D	49
68938-D	99
68986-D	126
68988/91-D	47
69047/8-D	120
69057/8-D	58
69095/6-D	124
69103/5-D	97
69142/3-D	51
69173/4-D	48
69180-D	113
69187/9-D	109
69213/5-D	90
69266/8-D	79
69326/7-D	122
69400-D	83
69410-D	127
69413/14-D	125
69470/2-D	91
69576/9-D	108
69600-D	60
69689/90-D	54
69737/40S-D	94
69822/45-D	93
70073/5-D	81
70338-D	116
70352-D	85
70365-D	88
70370/1-D	72
71036/8-D	118
71115/7-D	96
71135/7-D	73
71194/8-D	119
71250-D	59
71277/81-D	71
71329/30-D	106
71369/71-D	95
71439-D	117
71492/4-D	86
71583/5-D	92
71606-D	38,58
71620-D	88

70

NUMERICAL INDEX

Columbia

71621-D	83
71622-D	99
71623-D	49
72637-D	91
72962/3-D	240
72964/5-D	243
73048-D	290
73051-D	241
73052-D	242
73053-D	302
73054-D	303
73055/7-D	288
A-333	240
A-5808	11
AAL-5	241,242
AAL-6	302,303
AAL-7	281,282
AAL-11	259,292
AAL-27	240,293
BM-13	132
BTA-119/21	366
C-1002	290
C-1006	283
C-1008	297
C-1017	266,269
C-1018	298
CB-1	241,281,282, 292,293,303
CB-21	249,295
CX-1019	250
CX-1037	240,243
CX-1038	276,286
CX-1039	249,295
CX-1062	248
CX-1067	273
CX-1068/9	267
CX-1085	300
CX-1086	247
CX-1087	272,291
CX-1104	277,278
CX-1105	275,288
CX-1112	260,264
CX-1307/8	355
CX-1363	348,377
CX-1429	326,327,360
CX-1450	308
CX-1462/3	366
D-1638	34
DX-88/103	36
DX-630/7	37
J-211	240
L-1001	10
L-1001R	42
L-1002	11
L-1011	13
L-1016	14
L-1020	12
L-1040	15
L-1075	16
L-1104	21
L-1105	18
L-1115	19
L-1132	17
L-1162	20
L-1227	23
L-1248	24
L-1811/12	27
L-1864/7	26
L-2018/35	37
L-2058	28

Columbia

L-2087	28
L-2096	33
L-2118	39
L-2150	45
L-2156	46
L-2160/3	25
L-2220/22	41
L-2294/5	30
L-2344	32
L-2345	38
LB-19	89
LB-20	75
LB-44	68
LX-186/90	44
LX-224	76
LX-255	105
LX-262/5	82
LX-282/5	98
LX-317/18	55
LX-339/40	107
LX-353	104
LX-369/70	56
LX-378	74
LX-386/8	87
LX-391/2	103
LX-402/3	70
LX-433/5	101
LX-481/2	121
LX-501	114
LX-505/7	80
LX-515/19	57
LX-523/6	102
LX-530	100
LX-541/2	52
LX-557	123
LX-570	49
LX-574	84
LX-586/9	47
LX-596	99
LX-601	126
LX-614	53
LX-636/7	120
LX-638/9	58
LX-645/6	124
LX-656/8	97
LX-666/8	109
LX-687/9	90
LX-697/8	51
LX-702/3	48
LX-704	113
LX-721/3	79
LX-732/3	122
LX-746	127
LX-747	83
LX-754/6	91
LX-768/9	125
LX-785/8S	108
LX-797/800S	94
LX-805	60
LX-823/4	54
LX-838/9	72
LX-851/3S	93
LX-856/8	81
LX-865	117
LX-867	116
LX-869/73	119
LX-879	85
LX-880	59
LX-884/5	106
LX-887/9	118

Columbia

LX-893	88
LX-894/6	86
LX-904/8	71
LX-911/13	95
LX-915/17	73
LX-920/2	92
LX-927/9	96
LX-1322	302
LX-1337/40	290
LX-1361/3	276
LX-1391/3S	244
LX-1399/401	268
LX-1438	303
LX-1458	292
LX-1499/501	277
LX-1502	264
LX-1517/19	288
LX-1554	242
LX-1557	307
LX-1584	282
LX-1587	284,290
LX-1592	259
LX-1600	275
LX-8747/50S	297
LX-8790/1	255
LX-8813/14	272
LX-8924/5	243
LX-8931/2	262
LX-8942/4	295
Modern Music Album 2	25
M-45	26
M-123	41
M-190	82
M-194	98
M-224	87
M-238	56
M-239	70
M-240	103
M-244	101
M-264	80
M-265	57
M-271	37
M-274	102
M-290	62
M-302	47
M-305	61
M-316	97
M-330	109
M-333	90
M-336	79
M-355	63
M-360	91
M-366	108
M-387	94
M-399	93
M-409	81
M-447	118
M-456	96
M-458	73
M-470	119
M-479	71
M-509	95
M-524	132
M-538	130
M-544	86
M-548	92
M-552	49,83,88,99
M-933	290
M-934	288
M-990	275

NUMERICAL INDEX

NUMERICAL INDEX

NUMERICAL INDEX

74

NUMERICAL INDEX - ALPHABETIC INDEX

Victor		World Record Club		World Record Club	
M-1321	230	SHB-20	58,86,88,90,91,92,	T-;ST-744	336,339,
M-1334	220		93,94,95,96,97,98		350,372,
M-1345	163	SH-133	111,112		381
M-1356	201	SH-147	B-83	ST-786/8	356
ND-372/3	188	SH-158/60	129	T-;ST-837	351,352,
MC-124	189	SH-207	110,112		355,366,
SRL-12-28	369	T-;ST-82/3	355		373
V-14	167	T-;ST-558	331,344,362,368,	T-;ST-909	360,377
			371,386	ST-1085	380,B50
World Record Club		T-;ST-596	343		
CJST-744	316	T-;ST-632	353		
CM-;SCM-78/9	359	T-;ST-664	382		

ALPHABETIC INDEX BY COMPOSER

Excerpts from larger works not subdivided except where an overture exists independently. All numbers are A- prefix unless otherwise indicated.

Addison: Carte Blanche B-74
d'Albert: Tiefland 6
Alwyn: Sym 3 B-60
Arnell: Punch and the Child 244
Arnell: Ode to the West Wind B-51
Bach: Christmas Oratorio 160
Bach: Phoebus and Pan B-90
Balakirev: Thamar 245
Balakirev: Sym in C 308,B-58
Balfe: Bohemian Girl B-41
Bantock: Fifine at the Fair 161,B38
Bantock: Pagan Symphony B87
Bax: Garden of Fand 162
Beecham, A.: songs 128
Beecham, T.(Arr.) God Save..B4,B69
Beethoven
  Concerto, piano, No. 4 163
  Coriolan Overture 246
  Sym 2 26, 47, 310
  Sym 3 247
  Sym 4 134, B64
  Sym 6 248
  Sym 7 311, B-2,B-74
  Sym 8 249
  Sym 9 B-55
  Fidelio (Complete) B-68
  Mass in C 309
  Ruins of Athens 310
Berlioz
  Corsaire Overture 164,251,313,B76
  Damnation of Faust 18,48,312,314,B29
  Francs-Juges Overture 251
  Harold in Italy 250,B57
  King Lear Overture 165,251,B50
  Roman Carnival Overture 18,49,251,B78
  Requiem B75
  Les Troyens complete B30
  Les Troyens exc. 50,135,253,316,
    317,B29,B64,B72,B76
  Te Deum 252
  Symphonie Fantastique 315
Berners: Triumph of Neptune 51,254
Bizet
  Arlesienne Suite 1 52,318,B65
  Arlesienne Suite 2 53,318
  Carmen complete 321,B13,B22,B23
  Carmen Suite 54,240,319,320,B19,
    B28,B78
  Fair Maid of Perth complete B59
  Fair Maid of Perth Suite 23,55,255
  Patrie Overture 322
  Roma: Carnival 323
  Symphony in C 324

Bloch: Concerto, Violin B-8
Boccherini: Overture in D 256
Boccherini: Symphony No. 3 B-9
Borodin: Prince Igor Dances 11,27,56,325
    March 13,28,125
    Overture 137
Brahms *Tragic Overture* A 258
  Academic Festival Overture 326
  Alto Rhapsody B-10
  Concerto, Piano, No. 1 B-84
  Concerto, Violin 257
  Song of Destiny 327
  Sym 2 57,328,B-56,B-72
  Sym 3 B-64
  Variations, Haydn Theme B-38
Chabrier: Espana 59,259, B-29, B-62
Chabrier: Marche Joyeuse 233,330, B-28
Chabrier: Gwendoline Overture 329,B53
Charpentier: Louise B-18
Cherubini: Le Due Journées B-33
Debussy
  Petite Suite 24, B-15
  Prelude to Afternoon of Faun 60, 332
  Printemps 166
  Enfante Prodigue 331, B-9, B-62, B74
Delibes: Roi s'Amuse 333, B76
Delius
  Appalachia 63,260
  Arabesque 64,261
  Brigg Fair 29,30,167,334, B-62
  Dance Rhapsody No. 1 171,172,173,B-7,
    B-38,B-63,B-73
  Dance Rhapsody No. 2 139, 174, 335
  Eventyr 61,262
  Fennimore & Gerda Intermezzo 62,334
  Florida Suite 335,B70
  Hassan 61,63,173,263,B76
  In a Summer Garden 62,266
  Irmelin 63,168,336,B39,B85
  Koanga 61,63,264,B-15
  Marche Caprice 170,334,B-43
  Mass of Life 66,175,267
  North Country Sketches 140,176,268,B72
  On Hearing First Cuckoo 33,177,178,334
  On the Mountains 179
  Over the Hills & Far Away 62,269,335
  Paris 61,270
  Piano Concerto 138,169,170,B-9
  Sea Drift 31,62,265,270, B-10
  Songs 32,67,180,186
  Song Before Sunrise 141,181,182,334
  Song of High Hills 183
  Songs of Sunset 65,184,337
  Sleigh Ride 334

ALPHABETIC INDEX

ALPHABETIC INDEX - VOCAL & INSTRUMENTAL ARTISTS

(A selective listing)

Acknowledgement for providing additions and corrections to the basic discography is made
to the following persons: Norman Morrison, Michael Gray, J.F. Weber, Denis Vaughan, Tom
Patronite, John Ardoin, Stanley H. Mayes, George A. Locke, Dale Reutlinger, Kenneth DeKay,
Brian Rust, Richard T. Foose, Andrew Guyatt, Charles Niss, Jack W. Porter, Paul Koernich,
and John Borrego; to anyone missed, our apologies. Please carry these corrections over into
your copy of the discography and file this sheet together with it, as any further supplements
will not be cumulative.

Page 1:   Note 3. Eva Turner could not have recorded ca. 1909, so this is spurious.
          Note 5. All Odeon recordings at 76 RPM.
Page 2:   Note 2. A-6034 is not a Beecham recording.
          Note 3. All Columbia records recorded @ 80 RPM.
          A-19. Place (a) before both American Columbia numbers.
Page 3.   A-22. Clara Butt, contralto.
Page 4.   A-27. Add: (b) Col. 50130-D. Col. 7138/9-M may be conducted by Wood.
          A-29A. Add: Delius: Brigg Fair WAX 4355-1,-2,-3,-4 20 Nov 28 unpublished
          A-30. in WRC SHB-32. Rec. in Portman Rooms
Page 5.   A-32. Add "The Violet" also under (a). All in WRC SHB-32; (e) only in HMV
          ALP 1870/1 and Ang. 3621B.
          A-33. in WRC SHB-32.
          A-35. In WRC SHB-32.
Page 6.   A-40. Note 2. Remainder of this set Brahms Academic Festival Overture-Mengelberg.
Page 7.   A-44. Recorded by Victor.
Page 9.   A-48. Change (a) to read (c) and vice versa before matrix numbers.
          Note 1. Beecham can be heard to say "I'm (he doesn't complete the next word, which
                   may be "much"), I'm most grateful."
Page 10. A-61. All in WRC SHB-32. Rec. Abbey Road Studio.
          Add Note 2. The new edition of Beecham's book "Frederick Delius" included with the
               WRC set includes a discography which, due to lack of time, could not be
               incorporated here at this time. For a more detailed listing of alternate
               takes of these recordings, we refer you to this publication, which will be
               included in the next edition of the discography.
          A-62. (a) also recorded 2 April 36. (c) recorded 2 Oct 36. All in WRC SHB-32.
          Recorded Abbey Road Studio.
Page 11. A-63. (b) also with Van der Gucht and Royal Opera Chorus. Recorded 28 Jul 38.
          (d) should be CAX 8189-2A. All in WRC SHB-32. Rec. in Abbey Road Studio.
          Existing test of CAX 8162-1 released in WRC SHB-32; rec. 7 Jan 38.
          A-66. Should read: Introduction to Part 2, No. 3 (1s); in WRC SHB-32.
          A-67. (a) in WRC SHB-32. Add (c) Klein Wenevil and I Brasil, CAX 8190, rec.
          11 Feb 38, in WRC SHB-32.
          A-68. Rec. 4 Oct 35; in WRC SHB-32.
          A-64A. Add: Delius: Hassan: Unaccompanied Wordless Chorus (London Select Choir)
               Test Take TT-1853, Rec. Nov 1934; in WRC SHB-32.
Page 14. A-96. Add: in Col. ML-4674.
          A-97. Add: Note 3: CAX 7927-3A issued also.
Page 16. A-111. (a)(b) in Turnabout THS-65059.
          Note 1. Side 8 of American Columbia set cond. Harty.
Page 17. A-112. (b)(f) in Turnabout THS-65059.
Page 18. A-120. in Electrola C177 0033.
          A-124. in EJS-444. (b)(2) in Rococo 5233.
Page 25. A-161. Add Note 3: probably recorded on tape.
Page 26. A-175. Should be Part 2. in WRC SHB-32.
          A-176. Add Note 3. Transferred to Columbia label and issued (see A-268).
          A-176A. Add: Delius: The Homeward Journey (Marjorie Thomas, contralto)
               2EA 13746, rec. 6 Apr 49. Unpublished.

The following abbreviations are used for recording locations for the Columbia and HMV
recordings to follow: (AR) Abbey Road (W) Walthamstow (K) Kingsway Hall (SW) Salle
Wagram, Paris

Page 38. A-244: rec. AR   A-245: rec. W   A-246: rec. W
Page 39: A-247: rec. AR   A-248: rec. AR   A-249: rec. AR   A-250: rec. K; in CBS 77395.
          A-251: rec. W; in CBS 77395 A-252: rec. Horney Parish Church; in CBS 77395
          A-253: rec. W; in CBS 61655; 1958 recording date doubtful
Page 40: A- 256: rec. W   A-257: rec. AR   A-258: rec. W   A-259: rec. AR   A-260: rec. AR
          A-261: rec. W   A-262: rec. AR   A-263: Rec. Oct. 23,29, 1955 in W   A-264: rec. AR
          A-265: rec. AR   Note 4: add: Two excerpts, Serenade and We take the Golden Road
          to Samarkand, from Hassan, were recorded by Beecham on Oct. 12 & May 29 respecticaly,
          by EMI for CBS, but apparently not issued.
Page 41: A-266: rec. AR   A-267: Rec. AR. See talks. A-268. Rec. 14 Feb 49 in AR.
          A-270: Change artists to read: Bruce Boyce, BBC Chorus, Leslie Woodgate, dir.
          Rec. W. A-271: Rec. W; in CBS 61660. A-272: Rec. K. A-273: Rec. AR A-274: Rec. W

Page 42. A-275: Rec. Prob. AR   A-277: Rec. AR   A-278. Rec. AR A-279: in CBS 61655. Recording date doubtful.   A-280: Rec. W; Recording date doubtful. A-281: Rec. Prob. AR. A-282: Rec. AR   A-283: Rec. AR   A-284: Rec. AR

Page 43. A-285: Rec. W A-286: Rec. AR   A-287: Rec. W A-288: Rec. Prob. AR A-289: Rec. W A-290: Rec. Prob. AR   A-291: Rec. K; in CBS 61655; 1956 date doubtful. A-292: Rec. Prob. AR

Page 44. A-294: Rec. W A-295: Rec. AR   A-296: Rec. W A-297: Rec. AR A-298: Rec. AR A-299: Rec. W; in CBS 61655 A-300: Rec. AR A-301: Rec. W; in CBS 61655 (excerpts only: Miranda; the Naiads, Storm); A-302: Rec. AR

Page 45: A-303: Rec. AR A-304: Rec. W A-305: Rec. W   A-306: Rec. W; A-307: Rec AR

Page 46: A-308: Rec. 26 Nov, 2, 6, 15 Dec 1956 in AR

A-309: Rec. 4,5,7 & 13 May, 27,29 & 30 Nov. 1956, 21 Apr 58 in AR

A-310: (a) Rec. 19,20,28 Mar 1957, 9.14/16/24,25 May 1956 in AR
(b) Rec. 28(?) & 29 Mar @ 9 Oct 1957 in AR

A-311: Mono rec. 10,12,13 Oct 57 in SW; Stereo rec. 20 & 22 Oct 1958, 14 Jul 59 in AR

A-312: Rec. 25 Mar 57 in AR

A-313: Rec. 7 Nov 1958 in AR

A-314: Rec. 25 Mar 57 in AR

A-315: Mono rec. 8 & 9 Nov 1957 in SW with remakes 14 Mar 58; Stereo rec. 30 Oct & 1 & 2 Nov 1959 in SW; released in Time-Life STL-1-140, STL-2-140

A-316: Rec. 19 Nov 1959 in AR

Page 47: A-317: Rec. 23 Mar 1957 in AR

A-318: Rec. 21 Sep 1956 in AR

A-319: Rec. 10-12 Jan 1958 in SW

A-320: Rec. 4-10 June 1958; recorded separately at Carmen sessions

A-321: Rec. 4-10 June 1958 & 1-6 Sep 1959 in SW; released in HMV SLS 5021 and cassette TC-SL5021.

A-322: Rec. 12 Oct 56 in AR.

A-323: Rec. 9 Oct 1957 in SW.

A-324a: Mono rec. 7 & 10 Oct 1958 in SW; Stereo rec. 28 Oct, 1&2 Nov 1959
b: Mono rec. 11 Jun 1958; Stereo rec. 1-4 Dec 1959; released in HMV SXDW 3022 (SW)

A-325: Rec. 10 Nov 1956 in AR

A-326: Rec. 10 & 29 Nov 1956 in AR

Page 48: A-327: Rec. 13 May & 30 Nov 1956 in AR

A-328: Rec. 7&8 May & 17 Sep 56, 28 Nov & 1 Dec 58; 7&8 May, 14 Jul, Aug & 19 Nov 59 in AR

A-329: Rec. 9 Nov 57 in SW

A-330: Rec. 23 Mar 57 in AR

A-331: Rec. 5 Oct & 23 Nov 59 in AR

A-332: Rec. 25 & 28 Mar 1957 in AR

A-333: Rec. 12 & 16 May 58 in SW

A-334: (a) Rec. 31 Oct 56; (b) Rec. 31 Oct 56 & 2 Apr 57; (c) Rec. 5 Nov 56; (d) Rec. 5 Nov 56; (e) Rec. 28 Mar 57; (f) Rec. 31 Oct 56; (g) Rec. 5 Nov 56 all in AR

A-335: (a) Rec. 12,19,21,22 Nov & 14 Dec 1956; (b) Rec. 2 Apr & 8 Oct 57; (c) Rec. 7 Nov 56, all in AR

A-336: Rec. 31 Oct & 7 Nov 56 in AR

Page 49: A-337: Rec. in mono & stereo 1 & 2 Apr 1957 in AR

A-338: Rec. 31 Oct 1956 in AR

A-339: Rec. 23 Nov 1959 as a test in AR

A-341: Rec. 1-4 Dec 1959 in SW

A-342: Rec. 1-4 Dec 1959 in SW

A-343: Mono rec. 4-5 Nov 1957; Stereo rec. 1-4 Dec 1959, both in SW

A-344: Rec. 19 Oct 56 in AR

A-345: Rec. 9 Oct & 3 Nov 1957 in SW

A-346: Rec. 5 Oct & 1 & 2 Nov 1959 in AR

A-348: (a) Rec. in stereo 17 Nov 1955; (b) Rec. in mono 17,18,19 Nov. & 15 Dec 1955 both in AR. Stereo tape of (b) incomplete.

Page 50: A-349: Two recordings; first Rec. 18,21,29 Nov 1956 (unpublished); second rec. 27 & 28 Mar & 1 Apr 1957 in AR

A-350: Rec. 23 Nov 1959 as a test in AR

A-351: Rec. 31 Oct 1958 in K

A-352: Rec. 23 Apr 1958 in AR

A-353: Rec. 26 & 27 Nov, 14 & 22 Dec 1956; 29 Mar & 2 Apr 1957; 15 & 18 Aug & 24 Nov 59 all in AR

A-354: Correct number is SER 5631/4.

A-355: Rec. 17,18,21,22,25 Nov, 15,17,22 Dec 1955, 1 Jan & 16 & 29 May 1956 in AR

Page 51: A-357: (a) Rec. 4 Oct 1957 (b) Rec. 4 & 5 Oct 57 (c) Rec. 5 Oct 57 (d) Rec. 5,6,10 Oct & 3 Nov 57 (e) Rec. 9 & 26 Mar 57 (f) Rec. 7 Oct & 4 & 5 Nov 1957 all in SW. 1958 dates doubtful.

Page 51: A-358: (a) Rec. 8 & 16 May 58 in SW; 5 Dec 58 & 30 May 59 in AR
                (b) Rec. 11 & 16 May 58 in SW; 11 & 16 Dec 58 & 2-4 May 1959 in AR
                (c) Rec. 12 & 16 May 58 in SW; 11 & 18 Dec 58 & 2-4 & 8 May 59 in AR
                (d) early version rec. 19 Dec 55 & 29 Mar 57; later version rec. 9 & 16
                    May 58 in SW; 16 & 18 Dec 58 & 2-4 May 59 in AR
                (e) Rec. 9 & 16 May 58 in SW; 16 & 18 Dec 58 & 2-4 May 59 in AR
                (f) Rec. 10 May 58 in SW; 18 Dec 58 & 7&8 May 59 in AR
                Rehearsal excerpts in B-81.
         A-358A: Lalo: Symphony in G minor: See Bizet: Symphony in C
         A-359: (a) Rec. 15,16,23 Apr & 31 Oct 1958 in K; released in HMV SXDW 3022
                (b) Rec. 23 Apr 1958 in K
         A-360: Rec. 17 & 18Dec 1955 in AR
         A-361: Rec in mono 9 Oct 1957 in SW
         A-362: Rec. 6 Nov 1958 in AR
Page 52: A-363: Rec. 6 Nov 1958 in AR
         A-364: (a) Rec. 15 May 1958 in SW and 8 May 1959 in AR
                (b) Rec. 18 December 1958 in AR
         A-365: (a) Rec. 22 Dec 1955 & 28 May 1956 in AR
                (b) Rec. 26 & 28 Mar 1957 in AR
         A-366: Rec. 9,11,14,16,17,18,24,25 May 1956 in K
         A-367: Rec. 23 Mar 1957 in AR
         A-368: Rec. 29 Mar & 2 Apr 1957 in AR
         A-370: Rec. 18 & 28 Mar & 10 Oct 1957 in AR
         A-371: Rec. 7 Nov 1958 & 19 Nov 1959 in AR
Page 53: A-372: Rec. 5 Nov 1958 in AR
         A-373: Rec. 5 Nov 1958 in AR
         A-374: Rec. 20 Oct 1958 & 23 Nov 1959 in AR
         A-375: Rec. 25 Mar 1957 in AR
         A-376: (a) Rec. 12 & 16 May 1958 in SW; 22 May 58 & 2-4 May 1959 in AR
                (b) Rec. 7 & 14 May 1958 in SW; 18 Dec 1958 in AR
                3rd movement from (a) in HMV ALP 1870/1 & Ang. 3621B; both in HMV (new
                reissue, number not to hand), and cassette TC EXE 184.
         A-377: Rec. in stereo 25 & 26 Nov & 15 Dec 1955 in AR; released on WRC ST-909
                and HMV Stereo tape BTA 104
         A-378: Rec. 25 Mar 1957 in AR
         A-379: (a) Rec. 18,19 Dec 1955   (b) Rec. 19 & 25 Nov & 18 Dec 1955; (c) Rec.
                21 & 25 Nov 1955, all in AR.   (a)(b) released on HMV SXLP 30179 &
                cassette TC-EXE180.   (b) also includes Death of Melisande.
         A-380: Orchestra is BBC Symphony.
         A-381: Rec. 15,17,18 Dec 1955 in AR; released in HMV SXLP 30179 & cassette
                TC-EXE180.
Page 54: A-382: Rec. 17 & 22 April & 23 May 1959 in K
         A-383: Rec. 23 Mar 1957 in AR
         A-384: Rec. 5 Oct & 19 Nov 1959 in AR(?)
         A-385: Rec. in mono 8 Oct & 3 Nov 1957 in SW; 16 Apr 1958 in K; portion exists
                in stereo.
         A-386: Rec. 7 Oct 1957 in SW
DV writes: It will be of interest to many collectors to know that Sir Thomas balanced
           on the Mono recording of many of the above discs, both Columbia and EMI, even
           as late as the Carmen. As there were two teams working in completely separate
           rooms, this means that quite often the stereo does not carry the exact balance
           he wanted, as, although the engineers did their level best to keep up with him,
           his last minute comments before a take often did not give the stereo technicians
           the time to come in and alter a microphone placing in time for the next take.
           In general the stereo placings for the period were much simpler than the mono
           pickups, but it means that quite often the woodwind are favoured in the mono
           in a way which Sir Thomas particularly liked. Many of the stereo recordings
           were then approved for release by Lawrence Collingwood or Victor Olof, who did
           their utmost to make sure that Sir Thomas' wishes were not betrayed, but
           sharp eared listeners will be able to note the differences.
Page 55: B-1: also released on UORC-234.
         B-4: Recorded May 12, 1937.
         B-6: Entire performance exists from 18 June. Act 2 Exists from 22 June, with
              Schoeffler and Branzell in subsidiary roles.
         B-8A: Verdi: Aida with Caniglia, Stignani, Gigli, Borgioli, Covent Garden 1939,
               released on UORC.
         B-8B: Smetana: Bartered Bride with Konetzni, Andreva, Tauber, Tessner, Krenn,
               Covent Garden, 1939.
         Note 2: Change to read "Entire concert exists at BASF, including Vaughan-Williams
                 Wasps Overture; Mozart 39th; Delius Summer Night & Cuckoo; Rimsky-Korsakov
                 Coq d'Or Suite, Dvorak 8th Symphony. "

Page 57: B-16: Released on Operatic Archives Set 1005.
         B-18: Released on MOP-1.
         B-22: Highlights in UORC-289.
         Note 2 (Added): The tape currently in circulation of B-20 is in reality the
                performance of February 6, 1943 conducted by Leinsdorf.
Page 58: B-26: Cast: Jobin, Albanese, Pinza, Singher, Browning, Votipka, Baker.
         Act 1 duet released on UORC-254.
Page 59: B-34: Studio broadcast on Dec 18 & 20, 1947. excerpts survive.
         B-34A: Busoni: Piano Concerto w/Mewton-Wood, Rec. Jan 3-4, 1948
         B-33: Recorded December 19 & 21, 1947.
         B-38: Note 4 added: A program exists on BBC X13677/9, including Mozart Symphony
                No. 29, Bax Garden of Fand, Brahms Haydn Variations, all works introduced
                by Beecham. Broadcast on the general Overseas Service on 30 March 1949.
         B-39: (b) Scenes only, with Thomas Round, Joan Stewart. Recorded ca. 1954.
                From BBC Television, introduced by Sir Thomas.
Page 61: B-58: Also recorded & exist from this concert: Boccherini Overture in D &
                Gretry Suite from Zemire et Azor
         B-52: Also recorded & exist from this concert: Finnish & English National Anthems
Page 62: B-63: May be B-73e.
         B-63A: BBC Studio Concert, Maida Vale, Dec. 21, 1956: Mehul: Symphony No. 2
         B-63B: BBC Studio Concert, Maida Vale, Dec. 23, 1956: Rimsky-Korsakov: Le Coq
                d'or Suite; Beethoven: Symphony No. 2
         B-63C: R.P.O. Concert, Dec. 25, 1956: Haydn: Symphony No. 93; Delius: Paris;
                Mendelssohn: Midsummer Nights Dream Overture; Strauss: Bourgoise Gentilhomme
Page 62: B-73: Date of Concert is Dec. 25, 1958, and also included (d) Saint-Saens
                Rouet d'Omphale and (e) Strauss: Rosenkavalier Suite. (a)(b) and (c) were
                in BBCTS 100141/4.
Page 64: B-75: Date of concert is December 13, 1959.
         B-77: Concert was given prior to Seattle Symphony concert, acc. to DR.
Page 65: Other films: "The First Gentleman" music by Berkeley, with R.P.O., 1948
                          Publicity film for L.P.O., includes short speech followed by
                          fragment of Tchaikovsky's "Polish" Symphony
Page 66: Talks: Delius' Mass of Life, in WRC SHB-22.
                  Delete "Desert Island Discs" from "Records I Like"
                  Opera in England, date is Aug. 7, 1951.
                  Anecdotes, date is Oct. 15, 1958.
                  Foyles Literary Luncheon, date is Nov. 9, 1959
                  Promotional talk om Delius' Mass of Life (Columbia recording), 1954
                  Promotional talk on La Boheme (RCA recording), 1956
         Interviews: About Delius, by Edmund Tracy, in WRC SHB-22
         Note 4 (Added): Beecham's recitation at Delius' funeral in 1934 was recorded
                  acc. to H. P-G, but has not been located.
Page 67: B-86: A tape of this work does exist, without dialogue. with Bournemouth
                Symphony, and Laport, Hamel, Senechal, Boulangeot, Mandikian, Ducheneau,
                recorded May 11, 1955
         B-90: Was not broadcast. Given in Philadelphia, Jan. 20, 1942.
         B-91: Entire 1939 season recorded, including a Tristan.

Program of four Beecham concerts with "Ford" (Detroit) Symphony Orchestra follows:
   27 Jan 1946, with Lauritz Melchior: Rossini: Scala di Seta Ov; Puccini: Tosca: Recondita;
   Berlioz: Trojan March; Tchaikovsky: Waltz of the Flowers; Wagner: Tannhauser: Finale Act 1
   (w/chorus); Delius: Hassan: Serenade; Grieg: Norwegian Dance #2; Wagner: Meistersinger:
   Preislied; Rimsky: Scheherazade: Festival at Bagdad; trad: Onward thee and fear not
   3 Feb 46, with Andres Segovia: Rossini: Gazza Ladra Ov; Ponce: Allegro from Concerto del Sur;
   Brahms: Gypsy songs; Castelnuovo-Tedesco: Tarantella; Mendelssohn: Sym. #5 Andante &
   Scherzo; Albeniz: Torre berneja; Offenbach: Barcarolle; Sibelius: Karelia March; trad:
   Faith of our Fathers
   10 Feb 46, with Dorothy Kirsten: Berlioz: Roman Carnival Ov; Handel: Elopement excerpts;
   Mascagni Cavelleria Excerpt; Bizet: Bohemian Dance; Rubinstein: Since first I met Thee;
   Landon: A Southern Song; Strauss: Vienna Life; Pleyel: Life of Ages
   17 Feb 46, with Robert Goldsand, pf: Thomas: Mignon Ov; Chopin: Finale, E minor concerto;
   Chabrier: Marche Joyeuse; Sibelius: Bolero from Hist. Scenes; Dowland: Awake Sweet Love;
   Jensen: Murmering Zephyrs; Morley: Now is the Time for Maying; Liszt: Dance of the Gnomes;
   Rachmaninoff: G minor Prelude; Rimsky: March from Antar; trad: Now praise we great men
This accounts for all of B-28, plus B-29(a) and four numbers on B-78 AFRS #178. Marjorie
Lawrence broadcast a Scotch Medley and Immolation Scene with the Bell Orch. under Voorhees on
11 Feb 46, one day later, and this may be the listing on AFRS #192. Dorothy Maynor (on B-28
Program #3) sand the Allelujah with Reiner & Ford Symphony on 14 Oct 45, so may not be Beecham.
Beecham did not give any Ford Symphony concerts until the four listed above, but did conduct
an "Invitation to Music" on WABC on 14 or 21 Feb 1946, consisting of the Overture to "Welles
Raises Kane" by Bernard Herrmann, and Balakirev's "Thamar." This was the only other broadcast
noted by Bill Collins in his research from the period October 1945 to April 1946.

P 37 - E
  ° Good old times Waltz!